THE FAIR LABOR STANDARDS ACT

THE FAIR LABOR STANDARDS ACT

WILLIAM G. WHITTAKER

Novinka Books
New York

Senior Editors: Susan Boriotti and Donna Dennis
Coordinating Editor: Tatiana Shohov
Office Manager: Annette Hellinger
Graphics: Wanda Serrano
Editorial Production: Vladimir Klestov, Matthew Kozlowski and Maya Columbus
Circulation: Ave Maria Gonzalez, Vera Popovic, Luis Aviles, Raymond Davis, Melissa Diaz and Jeannie Pappas
Communications and Acquisitions: Serge P. Shohov
Marketing: Cathy DeGregory

Library of Congress Cataloging-in-Publication Data

ISBN: 1-59033-516-3

Nova Science Publishers, Inc.
400 Oser Ave, Suite 1600
Hauppauge, New York 11788-3619
Tele. 631-231-7269 Fax 631-231-8175
e-mail: Novascience@earthlink.net
Web Site: http://www.novapublishers.com

Printed in the United States of America

CONTENTS

Summary		**vii**
Chapter 1	Most Recent Developments	**1**
Chapter 2	Introduction	**3**
Chapter 3	Minimum Wage	**7**
	General Policy Concerning the Minimum Wage	9
	General Demographics of the Minimum Wage Workforce	17
	Minimum Wage Legislation in the 107th Congress	21
Chapter 4	Overtime Pay	**31**
	Structuring Work Hours Regulation	32
	Legislation in the 107th Congress	35
Chapter 5	Child Labor	**47**
	Child Labor in the United States	47
	Legislative Proposals of the 107th Congress	48
Chapter 6	Legislating a *Living Wage*	**57**
Index		**59**

SUMMARY

The Fair Labor Standards Act (FLSA) is the primary federal statute in the fields of minimum wages, overtime pay, and child labor. In the 107th Congress, legislation has been introduced that would modify the Act in each of these areas and extend its minimum wage protections to the Commonwealth of the Northern Mariana Islands (CNMI). Pending proposals would alter wage/hour and child labor protection with respect to specified groups of workers.

Following several decades of discussion and research in academic and reform circles, Congress adopted the FLSA in 1938. It has undergone major amendment on eight separate occasions, in addition to periodic more minor adjustments. Currently, the general minimum wage is $5.15 an hour. In the 106th Congress, there were diverse efforts not only to raise the minimum wage but to revise a number of the other provisions of the Act as well. Many of these proposals have been revived early in the 107th Congress.

Currently, there are several proposals to raise the general minimum wage to $6.65 an hour after January 1, 2003. Other proposals would establish slightly higher or lower floors and different timetables. At least one proposal would raise the minimum wage and then index it. Other wage-related initiatives would (a) extend federal minimum wage protection to workers in the Northern Mariana Islands and (b) preclude the payment of sub-minimum wage rates to vision-impaired workers solely on the basis of vision impairment. (At present persons with disabilities, under Department of Labor certification, can be paid a minimum wage commensurate with their productivity-but with no other minimum.)

Also pending are initiatives that would reduce federal minimum wage protections or limit the federal role in sustaining minimum wage rates. One bill would permit the states to opt out of the federal system where they agree to establish a state minimum wage standard of $5.15 per hour and maintain coverage comparable to that under the FLSA. Once out of the system, they would not automatically be subject to any future increases in the federal floor. *Among other proposals* are bills: to exempt licensed funeral directors and licensed embalmers (employees of funeral homes) from both the minimum wage and overtime pay; to structure a new exemption for certain "inside sales" workers; to expand the existing exemption with respect to computer services personnel; to redefine the concept of "regular rate" to exclude various types of incentive pay when calculating overtime pay; to prohibit *forced* overtime work by certain healthcare workers; and to make certain other changes in the FLSA exemption structure.

Legislation has been proposed to make broad structural revisions in federal child labor law. Other proposals would limit the employment of young persons in traveling sales work and permit Amish youth to work in wood processing plants at age 14 (currently this work is deemed too hazardous for anyone under age 18).

Chapter 1

MOST RECENT DEVELOPMENTS

The Fair Labor Standards Act (FLSA) of 1938, as amended, is the primary federal statute in the area of minimum wages, overtime pay, child labor, and related issues. Numerous bills dealing with aspects of the FLSA were introduced early in the 107th Congress. No immediate action was taken on these proposals.

On July 31, 2001, the House Subcommittee on Workforce Protections conducted a hearing on H.R. 1602, legislation to redefine the "regular rate" for overtime pay purposes. On June 27, 2001, the House Subcommittee on Workforce Protections marked-up H.R. 2070 (Tiberi), a bill to exempt employers of certain inside sales workers from FLSA minimum wage and overtime pay requirements, and ordered the bill reported to the full Committee. On June 5, 2001, the Senate Committee on Energy and Natural Resources reported S. 507, a bill to alter immigration policy as it affects the Commonwealth of the Northern Mariana Islands (CNMI).

There are no expiration dates embedded within the FLSA, so Congress is under no obligation to act on labor standards legislation-though the declining value of the minimum wage could provide an impetus for action. If Congress does move in this area, several approaches are possible. It could take up a single proposal: for example, to increase the minimum wage or to alter the overtime pay requirements of the Act. It could bring together a series of proposed amendments to the FLSA and consider them as a package. Amendments to the FLSA are normally of some controversy. Broadening the score of FLSA legislation could reduce the likelihood that any measure in this area will ultimately be adopted. Some proposed changes in the FLSA, now under consideration, are viewed as "poison pills" by labor standards advocates. On the other hand, a broader agenda could widen support for more narrowly focused initiatives. Some have urged that wage/hour legislation be coupled with tax and other benefits for business.

Chapter 2

INTRODUCTION

The FLSA is an umbrella statute that deals with a series of labor standards issues. These fall, roughly, into three categories: *first,* minimum wage (Section 6 of the Act), *second,* overtime pay (Section 7) and, *third,* child labor (Section 12). Section 3 of the Act defines the concepts used throughout the statute and, thereby, limits or qualifies its wage/hour and child labor provisions. Section 13 provides a body of exemptions and/or special treatment of segments of industry and/or groups of workers. Thus, while the Act is often treated as an integrated unit, it can also be approached in terms of its three general component parts—and of individual sub-units of each.

Under the FLSA, Congress has established a basic minimum wage (now $5.15 per hour) that must be paid to workers covered under the Act. However, *this is not a single standard:* the level of the wage floor may vary from one body of workers to another with various exceptions and sub-minima built into the statute. Thus, one needs to think in terms of which minimum wage rate (reflective of coverage requirements) may be applicable and to which group of workers it should be applied. The Act also sets a basic workweek (generally, 40 hours) and mandates payment of overtime rates (1½ times a worker's *regular rate* of pay) for hours worked in excess of that weekly standard. And it regulates (or, in some cases, prohibits) the employment of children. But, as with the minimum wage, there are coverage variations with respect to overtime pay and child labor. Through the years, diverse provisions have been added that have affected both the scope and administration of FLSA requirements.[1] Through at least 70 years, the

---

[1] Several considerations should be kept in mind. *First.* Many states have state-mandated minimum wage, overtime pay, and related labor standards. These may be roughly parallel to

minimum wage (alone or with other wage/hour issues) has sparked partisan comment and assertion.[2] The issue has not been solely *whether* there is an appropriate federal role in wage/hour regulation (that continues to be debated) but *what that role ought to be.* At what level should the minimum wage be set? Should it be indexed? How broad should minimum wage coverage be? And, if there are exemptions (which there are), upon what foundation should they rest? For example, should *small firms* be able to pay their workers at a lower rate than *large* firms? Should wage rates be productivity-based or respond to the needs and personal lifestyles of the workers involved? As under current law, should the rate vary with the age of the worker-even where the work and productivity level among workers may be comparable? Or, might the wage floor depend upon the use a worker makes of his or her off-duty hours: i.e., student status?[3]

Speaking broadly, how should the overtime pay requirements of the Act be structured? Under current law, are such requirements sufficiently flexible? Should work hours regulation and overtime pay requirements be, in effect, a core labor standard associated with employment-protecting employees from overwork and abuse? And, if the overtime pay *penalty* (levied against employers) is intended to discourage overwork and abuse, should workers classified as "executive," "administrative," or "professional" be exempt from such protection? How ought such concepts as *executive, administrative* and/or *professional* be defined? To what extent should the overtime pay requirement be modified by economic considerations within particular industries: by industry structure, employer convenience and profitability, etc.? When calculating a worker's *regular rate* for overtime pay purposes (e.g., 1½ times a worker's regular rate), should only the base rate be taken into account? How should bonuses or incentive pay be treated for such calculations? Such issues have been the focus of recent legislative proposals.

---

the federal FLSA: they need not be-and, often, are not. *Second.* Not all workers are covered under the FLSA-or, for that matter, state wage/hour standards. These coverage patterns (including patterns of exemption) need to be taken into account when considering the potential impact of changes in wage/hour law. *Third.* Because of the variations in coverage (the exemptions and extensive administrative rules laid down by the agencies charged with wage/hour and child labor enforcement), it may be perilous to suggest who is (or is not) covered by the requirements of statute, how low a wage they can be paid, etc., unless one is aware of *all* of the employment-related factors affecting each case. Too many variables impact coverage to allow easy assessment.

[2] For example, in his Convention speech (August 14, 2000), President Clinton affirmed that, were the Democratic Party "in the majority" in the 106th Congress, "America would already have ...a minimum wage increase." *See New York Times,* August 15, 2000, p. A17.

[3] Under current law, there are special rates for youth workers, for full-time students who work no more than part-time, for disabled persons, etc. That these rates (except nominally in the case of the disabled) are related to productivity may not be entirely clear.

Child labor regulation presents other concerns. Should children work? At what age? Under what conditions? Are there types of work (i.e., in mines, factories, sawmills) that can be deemed, on their face, too hazardous for young persons below a given age? Where work is generally deemed too hazardous for children, might special exceptions be made for certain groups or categories of children: for example, where the children are Amish or of other religious faiths? What is the appropriate relationship between work by children and school attendance? Is non-hazardous work "OK" if it is pleasant and something children might like to do, but to be more rigidly limited where it is not fun and more like real work? If children are allowed to work, should special hours limitations be imposed: i.e., the number of hours per day or week and/or the time of the day or evening?[4]

This book is divided into three segments; generally following the structure of the Act.[5] It raises issues currently (or historically) a part of the debate over the FLSA and takes note of legislative proposals of the 107th Congress that deal with these questions. Finally, in footnotes, it will indicate other Congressional Research Service (CRS) products that expand upon the themes suggested here or that may be otherwise useful.

---

4 In 1995, for example, the Department of Labor (DOL) ruled that 14 and 15 year olds *could work* late into the evening in the sports industry (as support staff, not as players). No comparable provision allows for late evening employment of children in other types *of* non-hazardous work such as with computers, in food services, etc. See *Federal Register*, May 13, 1994, p. 25167; and April 17, 1995, p. 19336-19339.

5 The issues of pay .equity and/or comparable worth are dealt with in other CRS products. See: CRS Report 98-278, *The Gender Wage Gap and Pay Equity: Is Comparable Worth the Next Step?*, by Linda Levine; and CRS Report RL30902, *Pay Equity Legislation* in *the* 1 O~ *Congress,* by Linda Levine and Charles. V. Dale.

Chapter 3

MINIMUM WAGE

The first federal minimum wage statute (the FLSA) was enacted in 1938. Its coverage was largely limited to industrial workers engaged in interstate commerce. Retail, service and agricultural workers, generally, were not protected—nor were persons employed by state and local governments. On eight separate occasions through the years (see Table 1), the Act has undergone general amendment which normally included language dealing with overtime pay and/or child labor as well as with the wage floor. On numerous occasions, the FLSA has been subject to more narrowly focused single purpose amendment.

Over the years, amendment of the FLSA has resulted in a broadening of coverage. Amendments have often been contentious and conditioned by economic considerations and political compromise.[1] DOL has interpreted FLSA exemptions conservatively, assuming that coverage was intended unless a clear case could be made, rooted in legislative history or in statutory language, for limiting the protection afforded by the Act. Generally, expansion of coverage has been opposed by employers and supported by workers. Each side in this debate has assembled a body of advocates including academicians (mostly conformists), policy analysts, and persons from the media. The literature, pro and con, is extensive but by no means definitive.[2]

---

1 See *Congressional Record,* July 30, 1937, p. 7876. More generally, see CRS Report 89- 568, *The Fair Labor Standards Act: Analysis of Economic Issues in the Debates of* 1937- 1938, by William G. Whittaker.

2 FLSA coverage was significantly extended in the 1960s and 1970s. Since 1977, change has been restricted *largely* to increases in the basic wage rate and modification of existing FLSA provisions. See Norlund, Willis J. *The Quest for a Living Wage: The History 01 the Federal*

Table 1. Federal Minimum Wage Rates, 1938-2001

Public law	Effective date	Rate ($)
P .L. 75-718	October 1938	.25
(Enacted June 25,1938)	October 1939	.30
	October 1945	.40
P.L. 81-393	January 1950	.75
(Enacted October 26,1949)		
P .L. 84-381	March 1956	1.00
(Enacted August 12, 1955)		
P.L. 87-30	September 1961	1.15
(Enacted May 5,1961)	September 1963	1.25
P .L. 89-601	February 1967	1.40
(Enacted September 23, 1966)	February 1968	1.60
P .L. 93-259	May 1974	2.00
(Enacted April 8, 1974)	January 1975	2.10
	January 1976	2.30
P .L. 95-151	January 1978	2.65
(Enacted November 1, 1977)	January 1979	2.90
	January 1980	3.10
	January 1981	3.35
P .L.1O1-157	April 1990	3.80
(Enacted November 17, 1989)	April 1991	4.25
P .L. 104-188	October 1996	4.75
(Enacted August 20, 1996)	September 1997	5.15

The basic federal minimum wage is statutory. It will remain at its current level ($5.15 per hour, set through legislation adopted in 1996) until Congress takes specific action to alter it.[3] Again, Congress has no specific obligation to revisit the minimum wage and thus *may* leave it at its current level. But over the long term, congressional inaction could have the effect of *repeal through attrition:* fewer and fewer workers would likely earn the minimum wage (its value having been reduced through the impact of inflation) and the requirement, eventually, could become a dead letter.

Minimum Wage Program. Westport, Conn., Greenwood Press, 1997; and CRS Report 95-202, The *Federal Minimum Wage and Select Bibliography,* by William G. Whittaker.

[3] Though basic FLSA requirements are set in statute (29 U.S.C. 201 ff.), significant administrative discretion has been given to the Secretary of Labor. Thus, there has been developed a body of federal regulations (29 C.P.R. 510 ff.), often supplemented by DOL "opinion letters" that apply the Act's more general provisions to individual workplaces.

Conversely, Congress could index the minimum rate to rise or fall with fluctuations in the general economy and, thus, assure its constant value. Bills introduced early in the 107th Congress took a variety of approaches to the minimum wage issue.

Where states have a minimum wage requirement that is higher than that required by the FLSA (which is permitted), *the higher standard normally prevails.* (See Table 2.) In addition, the minimum wage for American Samoa is set through a commission appointed by the U.S. Secretary of Labor and has been; generally, lower than the otherwise applicable federal rate under the FLSA. In the Commonwealth of the Northern Mariana Islands (CNMI), the insular government currently exercises authority with respect to wage standards—an issue in contention in the minimum wage debate in both the 106th and 107th Congresses.

General Policy Concerning the Minimum Wage

For almost a century, scholars and policy analysts have examined the issue of minimum wage rates, coming to a wide range of conclusions. Thus, few questions in the more recent debate are new—though they are still raised and remain the subject of dispute. Even basic issues remain in contention. For example, policy aside, what is the likely impact of a change in (or failure to change) the minimum wage requirements of the FLSA? What would be the likely labor market and price impacts? How good are the data upon which judgments in these areas are based? A review of hearings, congressional floor debates, and the general minimum wage literature suggests certain questions that seem frequently to recur. Some of these are sketched below. There are also assumptions that have been implicitly a part of the minimum wage debate even where they may not have been formally enunciated.

Table 2. Status of State Minimum Wage Rates[a]

Jurisdictions with minimum wage rates *higher than* the federal FLSA		
Alaska	District of Columbia	Rhode Island
California	Hawaii	Vermont
Connecticut	Massachusetts	Washington
Delaware	Oregon	
Jurisdictions with minimum wage rates *at the same level* as the federal FLSA		
Arkansas	Michigan	North Dakota
Colorado	Minnesota	Oklahoma
Guam	Missouri	Pennsylvania
Idaho	Montana	Puerto Rico
Illinois	Nebraska	South Dakota
Indiana	Nevada	Utah
Iowa	New Hampshire	Virginia
Kentucky	New Jersey	West Virginia
Maine	New York	Wisconsin
Maryland	North Carolina	Wyoming
Jurisdictions with minimum wage rates *less than* the federal FLSA		
American Samoa	New Mexico	Texas
Georgia	Ohio	Virgin Islands
Kansas	Puerto Rico	
Jurisdictions with *no* state minimum wage requirement		
Alabama	Louisiana	Tennessee
Arizona	Mississippi	
Florida	South Carolina	

Source: U.S. Department of Labor, Wage and Hour Division, Employment Standards Administration, April 1, 2001.

[a] Coverage patterns vary from one jurisdiction to another. Some jurisdictions have a structured minimum wage system: i.e., different rates for various industries, sizes of firms, etc. The table refers to *the highest standard applicable* under the law of the jurisdiction. In some jurisdictions, the rate (but not necessarily the pattern of coverage) is linked to the federal FLSA

The Socio-Economic Context of Minimum Wage

The minimum wage is often presented as a mechanism through which to assist the *working poor:* usually non-union workers with few skills and little bargaining power. Some early advocates of a minimum wage viewed it not only as socially useful but, also, as economically useful: promoting socio-economic equity, providing a floor under wages, stimulating demand for goods and services, expanding employment and, with other measures, bolstering the general economy.[4] Some critics of the minimum wage, conversely, have viewed it as an inefficient approach to income redistribution—and an unjustified intrusion into the operation of *the free market.* They contend that minimum wage increases have an inflationary impact and impose an unnecessary burden upon employers and consumers. Such critics often view the wage floor as economically harmful, especially for the unskilled and new workforce entrants who, they say, may be priced out of the job market.

Economists and policy analysts continue to disagree about the impact of changes in the minimum wage and about what the effects of the minimum wage have been. The issues are both socio-economic and ideological and have changed little since the debates of 1937-1938.

What Do We Mean by *Minimum Wage?*

When people speak of a minimum wage, they often speak in terms of "a livable wage" or "a decent wage" or "a fair wage" or suggest that the working poor ought to be able to live "in reasonable comfort" and enjoy economic "dignity." Early in the century, it was common to speak of a "living, family, saving wage." But, when individuals use such terms, is there any reasonable assurance of a consistent meaning?

In statute, the minimum wage is clearly defined: $5.15 per hour for most (but not all) covered workers. The FLSA does not translate that dollar amount into social or human terms. Is $5.15 an hour actually a "livable wage"-and, livable by what standards? Does "reasonable comfort," for example, mean safe and adequate shelter with modest amenities? How are "safe" and "adequate" and "modest" defined?

Some may view "minimum" as the lowest wage an individual will accept (a "reservation wage") or the highest amount an employer is willing to pay. Some urge repeal of a legislated wage floor altogether—and define

4 Concerning early interest in the minimum wage and the economic theory upon which that interest rested, see Glickman, Lawrence B. *A Living Wage: American Workers and the Making of Consumer Society.* Ithaca, Cornell University Press, 1997; Paulsen, George E. *A Living Wage for the Forgotten Man: The Quest for Fair Labor Standards,* 1933-1941. Selinsgrove, Pa., Susquehanna University Press, 1996; and Moss, David A *Socializing Security: Progressive-Era Economists and the Origins of American Social Policy.* Cambridge, Harvard University Press, 1996.

the "minimum" as whatever rates are set by supply and demand in a *free market* economy: i.e., a "market wage."

How *Minimal* is Minimum?

Minimum wage debates contain frequent references to the "poverty level" for a family of two or three or more (see Table 3). If Congress intends the minimum wage to be set at a level high enough to move a family out of poverty (as some suggest), then some measurement of family size and of total household income is necessary in assessing the adequacy of the FISA minima. If, instead, the minimum wage is productivity-based (i.e., resting upon the contribution of the worker), then family size and non-wage income would seem irrelevant.[5]

Under current law, a minimum wage worker, employed full-time and full-year (40 hours per week for 52 weeks at $5.15) would earn $10,712. A full-time worker, under age 20 and paid at the statutorily permissible sub-minimum rate, could earn $8,840. After 90 consecutive days *with an individual employer,* however, his/her sub-minimum rate ($4.25 per hour) would ordinarily increase to $5.15 an hour.[6] These amounts are prior to any deductions and exclusive of any fringe benefits. Table 3 sets forth the level of earnings regarded as a poverty threshold, at various family sizes, for eligibility for certain federal assistance pro grams. The extent to which the poverty guidelines are realistic can be, and has been, debated. The guidelines have no *direct* connection with the federal minimum wage but they are frequently cited in discussions of the minimum wage and are used by some analysts as a measure of the adequacy of the wage floor.[7]

---

5 Some may argue that basing a wage rate on the *productivity* of the worker may be, itself, misleading since in large measure worker productivity is based upon the skills of management and upon management-controlled elements such as work organization, availability of appropriate equipment, morale, ambience, etc.

6 This suggests some of the problems in calculating minimum wage earnings. While a worker under age 20 can be paid $4.25 per hour through the first 90 consecutive days with any employer, his wage after 90 days would have to be increased to the full $5.15 per hour-unless he moved on to a second, third, or fourth employer, or dropped out of work for a. period of time and broke the "consecutive" days pattern. Were he a full-time student working no more than part-time, he would be covered by a different sub-minimum wage option. If he were disabled in some manner but employed under DOL certification, he could be paid at any rate found to be commensurate with his productivity-however low that might be.

7 This might raise a counter question: How realistic is the *poverty threshold* itself as a measure of the cost of sustaining an individual or a family whatever its size? The issue is complex and technical and has sparked extensive literature.

Since much minimum wage work is also part-time and/or part-year, estimating actual annual income for minimum wage workers may be problematic. Similarly, choosing a wage rate that will comport with the work patterns of minimum wage earners and still provide "a living wage" may prove daunting. Moreover, those earning more than the statutory minimum: typically receive fringe benefits in addition to cash wages: e.g., health insurance, a pension, etc. Under present law, the concept of a minimum wage is limited to a cash wage.

Table 3. Poverty Guidelines, All States and the District of Columbia (2002)

Size of family unit	Poverty guideline		
	States and District of Columbia	*Alaska*	*Hawaii*
1	$8,860	$11,080	$10,200
2	11,940	14,930	13,740
3	15,020	18,780	17,280
4	18,100	22,630	20,820
5	21,180	26,480	24,360
6	24,260	30,330	27,900
7	27,340	34,180	31,440
8	30,420	38,030	34,980

Source: V.S. Department of Health and Human Services. *Federal Register*, February 14, 2002. p. 6931-6933.

Note: For family units with more than eight members, add $3,080 for each additional member. For Alaska, add $3,850, and for Hawaii, add $3,540.

To Whom Should *Not Less Than* the Minimum Wage be Paid?

FLSA minimum wage requirements have always been subject to exceptions, sometimes excluding from coverage those likely to be the most poorly paid workers. Upon what basis has Congress included—or excluded—workers from minimum wage protection under the FLSA?[8]

[8] See, for example, discussion during the 1938 debate on the original FLSA *Congressional Record*, June 14, 1938, p.9257.

When a Member of Congress (or, that body collectively through legislation) speaks of the "minimum wage worker," to whom is reference made? Is the minimum wage worker viewed as a single individual? A parent? A *single* parent? The sole economic support for a family? A teenager? Is the FLSA minimum intended to be a wage floor for all workers, urban and rural-for employees only of large firms, or for those employed by small businesses as well? *Should any non-work or non-productivity factors be taken info account when setting the wage floor*-for example, age (a youth or a senior citizen), student status, family size, etc.? Whom does a legislator have in mind when setting the federal minimum wage at, for example, $5.15 per hour? Is that mental image consistent with the demographic reality of the minimum wage workforce?

Various social and demographic distinctions have been cited to justify minimum wage rate differentials. For example, the FLSA, under certain conditions, allows a full-time student "employed in a retail or service establishment, agriculture, or the institution of higher education that such student attends" to be paid a lower minimum wage than that required for a non-student (even for equal work)—so long as the student works only "part-time." The wage level, here, is conditioned less upon productivity than upon how the worker spends his off-duty hours: i.e., enrolled in academic course work. If he drops out of school but keeps his job, the law requires that his hourly rate of pay be raised to at least the full applicable minimum. Similarly, even while remaining an employed full-time student, if his hours of work increase to more than part-time, he must be paid at the full applicable minimum rate. Applicability of the student sub-minimum rate (Section 14(b)) is dependent upon maintenance of full-time student status and not more than part-time employment. What is the rationale for paying a part-time worker less, on a per-hour basis (here, a sub-minimum rate) than a full-time worker—for the same work performed under the same conditions and equally well? What assumptions about "need" and "productivity" are implicitly built into the student sub-minimum wage option – and are these assumptions valid?[9]

Some may argue that younger persons, by definition, are less experienced and, therefore, less productive than "prime age" adults. This conclusion, however, *may not be valid for minimum wage-type work* and, indeed, an argument can be made that for low-skilled entry-level positions,

---

9 Some might argue that this creates an incentive for young persons to drop out of school or to shift their primary focus from study to work. The rationale for sub-minimum wage treatment, however, is that it may offset the problems young persons have in finding work that will match their academic schedules: i.e., by making them cheaper to employ.

young persons may be more productive: i.e., more vigorous, more nearly satisfied with such routine activity. What criteria should be taken into account with respect to the elderly (who *may* be less productive in minimum wage-type work) or for the disabled?

In short, should wages be needs-based or productivity-based? If a worker has an affluent spouse (or parents), should he (or she) be payable at *a sub-minimum* rate because his (or her) combined *family income* is relatively high? Should one who spends his wages for luxury items (tennis shoes, CD's, etc.) be paid at a lower rate than one who spends his earnings for tuition, baby formula, or elder care? If needs-based, then should the minimum wage be pegged to family size: the *more* children, the higher the minimum wage rate? Are such distinctions useful or workable and do they lend themselves to public policy formulations?

Who Should Pay the Minimum Wage?

How the minimum wage worker is defined and the intent of Congress in establishing/maintaining a federal minimum wage are critical to a consideration of by whom the minimum wage ought to be paid.

Is the minimum wage intended to be sufficient *to sustain a worker* (however defined by Congress): i.e., a single person without dependents or a sole breadwinner for a family? If so, should *an employer* be obligated to pay a wage of at least the amount needed to sustain the worker (and, where applicable, his dependents)-an amount that could, presumably, be affected by the assumptions built into the definition of *a minimum wage worker?*[10]

If a productivity-based minimum wage is not sufficient to sustain a worker (and his or her dependents, if any), then by whom should the deficiency be made up? Should it be paid by the employer who directly benefits by paying low wages (through utilizing the services of a low-wage workforce)-and, indirectly, by the consumer of the goods and services such low-wage workers provide? Or, should the difference between one's wage and need *be subsidized by* the taxpayer?

In 1975, Congress established the Earned Income Tax Credit (EITC) which, as amended, provides a tax credit to certain low-wage workers. Some laud the EITC for helping "to lift ...working families above the poverty

[10] Since workers compete with each other in the labor market, paying a needs-based rate could encourage an employer to hire single persons without dependents and, thus, to keep labor costs (wages) low: to avoid hiring persons who are married with children, etc.

threshold and to provide a greater work incentive to low-income workers."[11] But, the EITC can also be viewed as a subsidy, not only to workers but also to low-wage employers who may continue to pay low wages to their workers and to profit from utilization of such low-wage employees while tax revenues (through the credit mechanism, or through other public subsidies) assist their workers in meeting basic living costs. Thus, arguably, the routine cast of doing business is shifted from the individual employer to the taxpayer. Similarly, the EITC can be viewed as a subsidy to the consumers of the goods and services produced by low-wage workers.

Conversely, some argue, the EITC affords firms that operate on a slim margin an opportunity to remain in business and to provide employment, even if at low wages. However, the EITC is conditional upon the low earnings of the worker, not the marginal profit ability of the employer. It makes no distinction between businesses (employers) that are struggling economically and those that are doing well. Speaking generally, some view the EITC *as a supplement to* the minimum wage, predicated upon the needs of a worker rather than upon his productivity; others, *as a substitute for* future minimum wage increases. Employer/business acceptance of the EITC and hostility toward the minimum wage *may* reflect an economic reality: with the EITC, the taxpayer subsidizes the employer's wage costs; with the *minimum* wage, those costs fall directly upon the employer or businessperson and indirectly upon the consumer.[12]

As a related matter, the Act's small business exemption allows certain qualifying employers to be exempt from the FLSA minimum wage requirements. In general (though the exemption is complex), this could include firms "whose annual gross volume of business done" is less than $500,000, though individual employees of such firms, engaged in interstate commerce, may be covered individually. In addition, the Act contains numerous more narrowly focused exemptions.

Through the years, there has been pressure from the small business community to expand its exemption. Proponents have argued that small firms may be adversely impacted by having to pay their workers the minimum wage-or even driven out of business. However, some may argue that no test of profit ability has been proposed with respect to firms benefitting from the small business exemption: it is enjoyed by prosperous

---

[11] Bureau of National Affairs. *Daily Labor Report,* August 3, 1993, p. A10.

[12] Concerning the EITC, see: CRS Report 95-928, *The Earned Income Tax Credit (EITC): Effects on Work Effort,* by Jane Gravelle; CRS Report 95-542, *The Earned Income Tax Credit: A Growing Form of Aid to Low-Income Workers,* by James R. Storey; and CRS Report RS20470, *The Earned Income Tax Credit: Current Issues and Benefit Amounts,* by Melinda T. Gish.

and struggling businesses alike.[13] But, where small businesses are free from a minimum wage obligation, the question remains: How will workers employed by small businesses sustain themselves and, where applicable, their families? Further, what are the implications of a "small business exemption" with respect to competition between small firms and mid-sized firms?

GENERAL DEMOGRAPHICS OF THE MINIMUM WAGE WORKFORCE

Data concerning the minimum wage workforce are difficult to develop with precision. Some in the low-wage workforce may be paid at or below the federal minimum wage but, through exemptions built into the statute, may not be directly affected by the statutory rate. At the same time, some employers may choose to pay the statutory minimum because it is a convenient and generally recognized basic rate for low-wage employment-even where their workers may not be subject to the Act's minimum wage provisions. Further, persons employed at or below the federal minimum wage may change jobs (and economic status) with some frequency, moving in and out of work in response to non-work-related factors: school, pregnancy, a change in marital status, etc. Some may be multiple jobholders. And, not all workers *covered* under the FLSA are covered in precisely the same way. Thus, statistical data in this area may be a little imprecise and we may, often, be speaking of *the low-wage worker* rather than *the minimum wage worker.*

Who are the Minimum Wage Workers?

In 2000, about 2.7 million workers, paid hourly rates, earned at or below the federal minimum wage of $5.15 per hour: about 866 thousand were paid

[13] Much of the debate over increasing the minimum wage has focused upon the low-wage worker. Does he *really need* the increased income? Is he productive enough to justify (to earn) a higher minimum wage? Does he (or she) have other sources of income: for example, a working spouse or an employed parent? How will the worker spend his earnings: for essentials or for luxuries? But, comparable issues have not been raised about business. Does the small businessperson *really need* the increased profits from employing low-wage (sub-minimum wage) workers? Could he reasonably pay a higher wage? Or, is the employer's primary goal or motivation profit enhancement-at the expense of his employees and, under the EITC, of the taxpayer?

at the minimum rate and 1.844 million were paid *below* the minimum. These are workers who are 16 years of age or older.

In absolute numbers, according to data provided by the Bureau of Labor Statistics (BLS), persons working at or below the minimum are more likely to be *adults* than *youths,* more likely to be female, and more likely to be white.[14] Further, persons working at or below the minimum wage are more likely to be working part- time than full-time.

Critics of the minimum wage often point to a minimum wage worker who is a young person, walking for "pin money" and being supported by a suburban middle-class family. Conversely, proponents of a higher minimum often view the minimum wage workforce as largely adult and, *therefore,* suggestive of a more serious problem.

Statistics can be used to support either interpretation. If, for example, using 2000 data, one defines a youth as between 16 and 19 years of age, then about 31.2% of workers, paid hourly at or below the minimum wage, are youths and 68.8% are adults. If one's definition is more expansive, defining youth as between 16 and 24 years of age, then about 53.4% of persons earning at or below the minimum wage are youths and only 46.6% are adults. Thus, even with an expansive definition of youth (16 to 24 years of age), close to half of the minimum wage/sub-minimum wage workforce is 25 years of age or over. *For minimum wage type work,* however, the two demographic groups may well be in competition, with youth workers readily substitutable for older workers and with younger workers having an employment advantage: even where covered by minimum wage requirements, they can often legally be hired at a sub-minimum wage.[15]

Among hourly paid workers, at or below the general minimum rate, about 64.8% were women; about 35.2%, men. Although the data are imprecise because of "definitional questions with respect to race and ethnicity, about 82.7% of such workers may be classified as white.

In 2000, about 61.7% of those at and below the minimum wage were engaged on a part-time basis; about 37.8% as full-time workers. (Some statistical variation may result from a small number of multiple jobholders.)

---

[14] BLS divides the low-wage workforce into "white," "black" and "Hispanic origin" which may result in some double counting and some problems of racial/ethnic categorization.

[15] In addition to their legally allowable lower wage rate, other arguments can be made for the competitive advantages of youth workers. They may have more energy than older workers and may be more flexible. They are normally short-term employees who don't join unions, don't vest in pension programs, are less likely to be ill or suffer job-related strains that one might associate with long-term employment or age. Conversely, the argument can be made that they are less disciplined, have fewer skills (through few skills are required for minimum wage type work), are less dependable, and may be less acclimated to the culture of the world of work.

Low-wage employment may tend to be less stable than more highly compensated employment, with workers suffering involuntary joblessness or moving in and out of the labor force from discouragement, to seek better wages and working conditions, or for other reasons.

Full-time employment is not synonymous with full-year employment. Thus, estimating the annual income of minimum wage workers may be problematic since many full-time minimum wage workers may not be employed on a full-year basis. There may be periods when they are not working. (or not working at the minimum wage).

Beyond uncertainties about combinations of part-time or full-time, part-year or full-year employment, one must recall that the minimum wage is a cash wage. Fringe benefits earned by a minimum wage worker are likely to be less than those of more highly paid persons, widening the gap between the economic well-being of the minimum wage worker and others. On the other hand, minimum wage workers may have other sources of income.[16]

Estimating the Size of the Minimum Wage Workforce

In 2000, as noted above, there were roughly 2.7 million workers, paid hourly rates, who earned at and below the federal minimum wage of $5.15 per hour. They constituted only about 3.7% of hourly paid workers from an aggregate of about 72.7 million. This is the smallest aggregate number of persons earning at or below the minimum wage in over 20 years (see Table 4). An important question is: Why?

This numerical decline is not necessarily indicative of improved economic status for the low-wage worker. Rather, it may be that, as the value of the statutory minimum shrinks in terms of constant dollars, fewer workers are employed at or below the reduced rate-and those who are still so employed have experienced a relative reduction in their minimum wage earnings.

In policy terms, this would appear to have several implications. If the statutory minimum wage remains at its current level while the general wage level rises because of inflation, the number of minimum wage workers could reasonably be expected to experience a further decline. Fewer and fewer people could be expected to be employed at the low wage level. Thus, were

[16] Data, here, are drawn from an analysis, *Characteristics of Minimum Wage Workers: 2000*, prepared by the V.S. Bureau of Labor Statistics. BLS hag used data from the Current Population Survey (CPS), provided from the V.S. Bureau of the Census. Interpretive

Congress to take no action with respect to the minimum wage, allowing its value to continue to decline, the size of *the minimum wage workforce* could reasonably be expected to decline until it virtually disappears. This would not mean that the low-wage workforce bad shrunk: merely that an increasingly large number of such persons would be employed at wages above the statutorily defined minimum.

Table 4. Number and Percent 01 Workers Paid Hourly at the Minimum Wage or Less

Year	Workers paid hourly rates	
	Total paid the minimum wage or less	
	Number in thousands	As a percentage of hourly paid workers
1979*	6,913	13.4
1980*	7,773	15.1
1981*	7,824	15.1
1982	6,496	12.8
1983	6,338	12.2
1984	5,963	11.0
1985	5,538	9.9
1986	5,060	8.8
1987	4,697	7.9
1988	3,927	6.5
1989	3,162	5.1
1990*	3,228	5.1
1991*	5,283	8.4
1992	4,921	7.7
1993	4,332	6.7
1994	4,127	6.2
1995	3,655	5.3
1996*	3,724	5.4
1997*	4,754	6.7
1998	4,427	6.2
1999	3,340	4.6
2000	2,710	3.7

Source: United States Bureau of Labor Statistics.
(*) Years in which a legislated change in the federal minimum wage took effect.

questions associated with data collection may have some impact upon the precision of estimates presented here.

Under this scenario (which is generally consistent with the trajectory of legislated increases in the statutory minimum wage since 1968), the minimum wage would have been effectively *repealed by attrition.*[17] In that context, an argument might be made that, since so few would actually be employed at rates at or below the statutory minimum (its relative value notwithstanding), the problem of the working poor could be handled through other more narrowly targeted means-possible through transfers of income rather than through strictly work-related earnings. This, however, would run counter to recent public policy that income from work is generally preferable to transfers or entitlements.

MINIMUM WAGE LEGISLATION IN THE 107TH CONGRESS

Early in the 107th Congress, various proposals were introduced that would increase the federal minimum wage floor and/or make other changes in the FLSA. What approach Congress might take: with respect to labor standards legislation-or, for that matter, whether it would take any action at all-has not been entirely clear.

Establishing a *Tradition?*

The original FLSA proposals of 1937-1938 were in the form of free-standing legislation: focusing narrowly upon labor standards but covering the entire field of wage/hour and child labor protections. As a procedural matter, the next seven rounds of minimum wage increases (1949,1955,1961,1966, 1974, 1977, and 1989), though each provided for other changes in the FLSA, took the form of free-standing legislation. Non-FLSA or non-wage/hour issues were not addressed as part of a package with minimum wage and related concerns. Any "trade-off' to assist employers in dealing with the impact of wage/hour enactments (for example the "tip

[17] Were the minimum wage to have roughly the value that it had at its peak in 1968, the statutory rate would now be about $8.05 per hour rather than the current actual rate of $5.15. It may be significant that, of the measures pending in the 107th Congress, the highest minimum rate proposed is $6.65 per hour (to take effect only after January 1, 2003). See CRS Report RS20040, *Inflation and the Real Minimum Wage: Fact Sheet*, by Brian W. Cashell.

credit" and student sub-minimum wage provisions) were considered within the context of wage/hour) legislation *per se.*

In 1996, minimum wage and related FLSA amendments were brought to the floor in the House as an amendment to a broad package of non-wage/hour proposals. Indeed, the FLSA was a relatively small part of the overall package. While some components of the wage/hour portion of the bill bad been the subject of hearings during the 104th Congress, others bad not been-nor bad the body of FLSA-related provisions been considered by committee as a unit. During the spring and summer of 1996, the joint minimum wage/tax revision measure moved through Congress, being signed by President Clinton on August 20, 1996 (P .L. 104-188).[18]

When minimum wage legislation came to the fl oor during the 106th Congress, it largely followed the 1996 pattern. It combined tax revisions in behalf of the business community with changes in the FLSA-including an increase in the minimum wage.[19] By the 106th Congress, the two-a minimum wage increase and tax breaks for employers-bad become linked: i.e., that the former could not go forward, *it* seemed, without the latter.

Linkage, although a *tradition* only since the 104th Congress, appeared to be the essential focus of the legislative debate of the 106th Congress. "We came to the table," observed Representative Lazio, "with the realization that a wage increase was fair but we also came to the table with a desire to protect the small business people who will end up bearing the direct burden of any wage increase that we pass here today."[20] Senator Nickles concluded, looking ahead to the 107th Congress: "It kind of fits, frankly, to do it as apart of the tax package next year."[21]

However, not all concurred. Amy Borrus, writing in *Business Week,* termed the tax/minimum wage bill "a monument to legislative logrolling," stating that "its veneer of virtue made it the perfect vehicle for a tax-break

---

[18] See CRS Issue Brief 1B95091, *The Minimum Wage: An Overview o[Issues Before the 104th Congress,* by William G. Whittaker (archived, but available from the author). See also: Rubin, Alissa J. Congress Clears Wage Increase with Tax Breaks for Business, *Congressional Quarterly,* August 3,1996, p. 2175-2177; and Kosterlitz, Julie. A Bounty For Business, *National Journal,* October 26, 1996, p. 2289-2292.

[19] In the Senate, minimum wage increases bad been included within H.R. 833, as amended, the Bankruptcy Reform Act of 1999; in the House, it was part of H.R. 3081, the "Small Business Tax Fairness Act of 2000." Though each house passed aversion of the minimum wage legislation, the proposals died at the close of the 106th Congress. See CRS Report RL30690, *Minimum Wage and Related Issues Before the 106th Congress: A Status Report,* by William G. Whittaker.

[20] *Congressional Record,* March 9, 2000, p. H860.

[21] Bureau of National Affairs. *Daily Labor Report,* December 6, 2000, p. A12.

extravaganza."[22] Representative Rangel seemed to sum up the views of critics of linkage: "We should not be forced to bribe the wealthy in our society in order to secure a simple dollar more per haut for the poorest working American families."[23]

Some action on the minimum wage and related issues may be likely during the 107th Congress-but it is by no means assured. Nor is it clear whether linkage will gain be the focus of the debate. Several FLSA-related bills were introduced early in the first session; others appear to be under discussion.[24]

Proposals to Alter the Minimum Wage Requirement

Because the minimum wage under the FLSA is set in statute, it remains at a fixed level, without regard for changes in the general economy, until Congress alters it through legislation. Various changes in the wage floor-at large and with respect to certain targeted groups of workers-have been proposed. While most would raise the minimum wage, some could result in payment at lower rates.

In 1938, the federal minimum wage rate was set at 25 cents per hour. Its real value has fluctuated through the years reaching a peak in 1968 and, thereafter, declining. *To equal its 1968 value, the minimum wage would now (fall 2001) need to be about $8.05 an hour-$2.90 above its current statutory level of* $5.15 *per hour.*[25]

---

22 Borrus, Amy. Why Business Isn't Bucking This Minimum-Wage Hike, *Business Week,*November 1, 1999, p. 55. Borrus added: "And that's how lobbyists managed to squeeze maximum benefits for their clients out of the Ini l rimum-wage measure."

23 Bureau of National Affairs. *Daily Labor Report,* March 9, 2000, p. A8.

24 In general, see: Bureau of National Affairs. *Daily Labor Report,* April 25, 2001, p. A6- A7; and Eilperin, Juliet. Business Seeks Tax Breaks in Wage Bill: Pay Raise is Viewed as Best Chance at Cuts, *The Washington Post,* May 14, 2001, p. A1 and A12. In an article, Business Coalition Holds Firm for Bush Tax Cut Package, *Congress Daily,* April 19, 2001, reporters Stephen Norton and Charlie Mitchell state that trade association and business supporters of the Bush Administration's tax package have shown "remarkable discipline in resisting the urge to press for inclusion of their own pet items" in the tax package, "mindful of assurances from GOP leaders that there will be a 'second bite at the apple' for business- specific provisions next year or even later this year-possibly paired with a bill to raise the minimum wage."

25 See CRS Report RS20040, *Inflation and the Real Minimum Wage: Fact Sheet,* by Brian W. Cashell; and CRS Report 98-960, *The Federal Minimum Wage and Average Hourly Earnings 01 Manufacturing Production Workers,* by William G. Whittaker. Of currently pending proposals, only H.R. 2812 (Sanders), it seems, would restore the federal minimum wage to its 1968 value.

Representative Traficant early introduced legislation (H.R. 222) that would raise the minimum wage in two steps: to $5.65 per hour after July 1, 2001, and to $6.15 per hour after July 1, 2002. The Traficant bill would make no other changes in current law. He subsequently introduced two other bills with the same purpose: H.R. 2241 and H.R. 2424-the latter, a two-step series of increases raising the wage rate to $6.77 per hour. S. 277 (Kennedy) and H.R. 665 (Bonior) would raise the minimum wage in three steps: to $5.75 "30 days after the date of enactment," to $6.25 after January 1, 2002; and to $6.65 after January 1,2003. The Kennedy and Bonior bills both extend federal minimum wage coverage to the Commonwealth of the Northern Mariana Islands (CNMI). The rates for the island group would be phased-in, beginning with a floor of $3.55 per hour "30 days after the date of enactment" and then, at 6-month intervals, increasing by 50 cents an hour until the general federal rate is reached. On May 25, 2001, Senator Kennedy reintroduced his minimum wage proposal, S. 964. This latter proposal also contains the Mariana Islands provision.

In separate action, Senator Dodd introduced S. 940, entitled *"A Bill To Leave No Child Behind."* An umbrella proposal, it deals with a variety of socio-economic pro grams and, *inter alia,* would raise the minimum wage, in steps, to $6.65 an hour after January 1, 2003, and extend minimum wage coverage to the CNMI-as provided in S. 277, H.R. 665, and S. 964. See also H.R.1990, companion legislation introduced by Representative George Miller.

S. 8 (Daschle) provides for a general minimum wage increase (in three steps, the same as the Kennedy and Bonior bills) and extends minimum wage coverage to the CNMI under the same formula as in the Kennedy and Bonior bills. It makes no other changes in the FLSA. However, the Daschle bill, titled the *"Enhancing Economic Security for America's Working Families Act,* "includes a lengthy series of non-FLSA provisions that deal with "pay equity," lifelong learning, tax relief for working families, and related matters.

H.R. 546 (Quinn) would raise the minimum wage to $5.65 per hour after April 1, 2001, and to $6.15 per hour after April 1, 2002.[26] The Quinn bill would also make-other changes in the FLSA. It would: *first,* expand the current pattern of wage/hour exemption (special treatment) for computer professionals; *second,* exempt from minimum wage and over time pay certain sales employees, and, *third,* exempt from minimum wage and

[26] Where a target date in a bill hag been passed prior to legislative action, the date is normally altered to reflect the impact of such passage of time.

overtime pay licensed funeral directors and licensed embalmers. Further, the Quinn bill, titled the *"Small Business Tax Fairness Act of 2001,"* provides a series of business-related changes in tax law, with other provisions.[27] On June 7, 2001, Representative Quinn introduced H.R. 2111, a bill by the same title but of different substance. Though it still contains non- FLSA provisions, the only change it would mandate in the FLSA would be to raise the minimum wage to $5.65 per hour after September 1, 2001, and to $6.15 per hour after April 1, 2002.

Other bills deal with aspects of minimum wage and/or overtime pay coverage under the FLSA H.R. 648 (Graham) is a free-standing proposal to exempt from minimum wage and overtime pay requirements employers of licensed funeral directors and licensed embalmers. A parallel proposal, H.R. 3678 (Graham), would exempt from minimum wage and overtime pay requirements employers of "certain construction engineering and design professionals," defined in the legislation. H.R. 3486 (Ballenger) would amend Section 3(f) of the FLSA to include within the definition of "agriculture" the growing, cultivation, etc., of "Christmas trees." H.R. 2070 (Tiberi) would alter the minimum wage and overtime pay treatment of certain sale's employees. (See discussion under overtime pay issues, below.) H.R. 2679, the "Camp Safety Act of 2001," introduced by Representative Andrews, would create an exemption from both minimum wage and overtime pay requirements of the FLSA for an "organized camp" that complies with certain safety and health standards specified in the legislation.

H.R. 881 (Isakson; see discussion below) would prohibit the payment of a sub-minimum wage to persons who are vision-impaired based solely upon that impairment. Currently, under Section 14(c) of the FLSA, workers with disabilities can be paid (with DOL certification) at a sub-minimum rate that is commensurate with their productivity-but with no floor. Under H.R. 881, persons with multiple disabilities could still be subject to DOL-certificated sub-minimum wage employment.[28]

---

27 See: CRS Report RL30537, Computer Services Personnel: Overtime Pay Under the Fair Labor Standards Act; CRS Report RL30003, Modifying Minimum Wage and Overtime Pay Coverage for Certain Sales Employees Under the Fair Labor Standards Act; and CRS Report RL30697, Funeral Services: The industry, Its Workforce, and Labor Standards, all by William G. Whittaker.

28 For a discussion of this issue, see CRS Report RL30674, *Treatment 01 Workers with Disabilities Under Section* 14(c) of *the Fair Labor Standards Act,* by William G. Whittaker.

Indexation of the Minimum Wage

When minimum wage legislation became an issue early in the 20th century, one consideration was how it ought to be structured. Should it be a fixed rate, or might it usefully be indexed to reflect changes in the cost of living (or shifts in other economic variables)? Indexation has remained, intermittently, an issue, and was a subject of extensive debate during the 1970s.

On August 2, 2001, Representative Sanders introduced H.R. 2812. The bill, titled the "Minimum Wage Restoration Act," would raise the minimum wage, in steps, to $8.15 per hour after January 1, 2003, roughly the equivalent value it bad in 1968. Beginning in 2004, the minimum wage would be adjusted each year to reflect changes in the cast of living.[29]

State Flexibility/State's Option

During the 1937-1938 debates on the original FLSA legislation, it was argued by some employers, especially from low-wage areas of the country, that a system of regional or other differentials should be built into the Act. Congress, fearing inter-regional wage-based competition that could result in a downward economic spiral, rejected the concept-opting instead for a national wage *floor* in covered work.[30] Some, however, have continued to urge creation of regional/state sub-minima. States, of course, are free to adopt standards higher than those set by Congress and many have.

In the 106th Congress, Representative DeMint introduced legislation that would have allowed individual states to preempt the federal minimum wage under the FLSA so long as the state rate did not fall below $5.15 per hour (without regard for any higher federal rate that might subsequently be legislated).[31] A companion bill was introduced by Senator Enzi. Although the DeMint proposal was free-standing, its substance was added to umbrella tax/labor standards legislation under consideration in the House during the 106th Congress-but dropped before that measure was called up for final vote

---

29 See: CRS Report RL30927, *The Federal Minimum Wage: The Issue of Indexation*, by Gerald Mayer.

30 Though many, in 1937 and 1938, bad urged setting the minimum wage at 40 cents an hour, Congress compromised at 25 cents an hour-basically a concession to the low-wage sections of the country.

31 There were other elements incorporated in the DeMint bill: the bill passed through several versions.

in the House. The House-passed tax/labor standards measure died at the close of the 106th Congress- as did the free-standing DeMint and Enzi bills.

The industry-oriented Employment Policies Institute has urged adoption of the DeMint/Enzi flexibility approach, arguing that the current "one-size-fits all" national standard "does not make sense." It observed: "Governors should be given the opportunity to act as they see fit with regard to local labor markets, without the burden of a federal mandate [the minimum wage] that ignores all local labor market conditions."[32] Similarly, the concept has won approval from the Heritage Foundation's Mark Wilson[33] and is said to have the support of Labor Secretary Elaine Chao and President Bush. Others regard the initiative as a veiled means of gutting the FLSA and of effective repeal of the *federal* minimum wage. Some observe that if state flexibility is included in minimum wage legislation, it could spark a filibuster. A spokesperson for Senator Kennedy reportedly branded it as one of a number of "poison pills" and "a total nonstarter" legislatively.[34]

In the 107th Congress, Representative DeMint (with Representatives Stenholm and Armey) has reintroduced state flexibility legislation (H.R. 1441). It would allow states where the state mininlum wage is at least $5.15 per hour and coverage is comparable to federal law to opt out of future FLSA minimum wage increases.

Commonwealth of the Northern Mariana Islands (CNMI)

In the mid-1970s, the CNMI entered into a quasi-autonomous relationship with the United States. By the Commonwealth agreement, regulation of overtime pay, under the PISA, is enforced by DOL. CNMI law governs the minimum wage. In addition, the CNMI controls its own immigration policy. Further, the CNMI is regarded as within the V.S. customs area. The result has been the development of industry based upon low wages and alien contract labor, the product of which carries a "Made in America" label and competes with other American-made goods.[35]

---

32 See Employment Policy Institute. *State Flexibility*, July 1999. Downloaded from: [epionline.org], October 25,1999.

33 Wilson, Mark D. *Successful Welfare Reform Requires State Flexibility on the Minimum Wage*. The Heritage Foundation Executive Memorandum No. 625, September 20, 1999. Downloaded from: [epionline.org], August 22, 2000.

34 Bureau of National Affairs. *Daily Labor Report*, April 18, 2001, p. CC1-CC2 and C1.

35 See CRS Report RL30235, Minimum Wage in the Territories and Possessions of the United States: Application of the Fair Labor Standards Act, by William G. Whittaker.

Through the past decade, human fights and labor standards in the CNMI have been the subject of DOL investigations, congressional hearings, and proposed legislation. In the 105th Congress, the Committee on Energy and Natural Resources voted to report legislation co-sponsored by Senators Akaka and Murkowski that would, *inter alia,* have created a U.S. controlled insular minimum wage structure.[36] The legislation died at the close of the 105th Congress, but the CNMI issue was the subject of further hearings by the Committee during the 106th Congress. During the 106th Congress, several general minimum wage proposals included language that would have brought the CNMI wage floor into conformity with that of the states.

In the 107th Congress, there is continuing interest in the CNMI. S. 8 (Daschle), S. 277 and S. 964 (Kennedy), and H.R. 665 (Bonior) would each extend federal minimum wage protection to workers employed in the CNMI- but would phase-in the full national rate through a series of incremental steps. Subsequent bills contain the same provisions with respect to the CNMI: S. 940 (Dodd) and B.R. 1990 (George Miller). On July 26, 2001, Representative George Miller introduced B.R. 2661, the "United States-Commonwealth of the Northern Marianas Human Dignity Act." Among other provisions, H.R. 2661 would require that CNMI-produced goods labeled "Made in USA" would need to have been produced at not less than the minimum wage rate under the- FLSA The legislation provides for an initial rate not less than $3.55 per hour with a gradual phasing-in of the full FLSA minimum rate.

In related action, on June 5, 2001, the Senate Committee on Energy and Natural Resources reported S. 507 (Murkowski), a proposal to amend immigration law as it applies to the CNMI under the Covenant of association between the Islands and the United States. (See S.Rept. 107-28.)

Minimum Wage Treatment of the Blind

Under Section 14(c) of the FLSA, persons with various physical and/or mental disabilities can be employed at wage rates below the otherwise applicable federal minimum wage. Under certificates issued by the Secretary of Labor, their wages are set at a level *commensurate with* their productivity and ret1ective of rates found to be *prevailing* in the locality for essentially

[36] U.S. Congress. Senate. Committee on Energy and Natural Resources. *Northern Mariana Islands Covenant Implementation Act, Report To Accompany* S. 1275. 105tb Cong., 2nd Sess., S.Rept. 105-201.

"the same type, quality, and quantity of work." For these workers, under current law, *there is no statutory minimum wage rate.*

The exemption goes back, in one form or another, at least to the National Industrial Recovery Act (NIRA) of the early 1930s-thereafter being incorporated within the FLSA (1938). The precise manner of treatment (and of compensation) for the targeted workers has varied through the years. During certain periods, certificated workers were paid a *sub-minimum* rate and were segregated according to the severity of their disabilities, with the most severely disabled placed in "work activities centers." In 1986, Section 14(c) was amended to remove the separation of workshops for the disabled from the work activities centers-and to eliminate any statutory wage floor for persons with disabilities in certificated employment. In 1994, further hearings were conducted amid charges by some that the system of productivity-based sub-minimum wage rates for persons with disabilities was inequitable and unworkable. The law, however, supported by employers of such workers, was not altered.

Since the mid-1990s, bills have repeatedly been introduced that would change current law and practice. On March 6, 2001, Representative Isakson introduced H.R. 881, which, if adopted, would prevent the Secretary of Labor from issuing a certification for the payment of a sub-minimum wage to persons who are vision-impaired solely on the basis of vision impairment; other factors would need to be taken into account. The bill would not prevent the issuance of such certificates where potential workers have multiple disabilities, one of which may be vision impairment.[37]

---

[37] For a discussion of the Section 14(c) program, see: CRS Report RL30674, *Treatment of Workers with Disabilities Under Section* 14(*c) of the Fair Labor Standards Act,* by William G. Whittaker; and V.S. General Accounting Office. *Special Minimum Wage Program: Centers after Employment and Support Services to Workers with Disabilities, But Labor Should Improve Oversight.* Report to the Congress, Comptroller General of the United States. GAO-01-886, September 2001. Washington, Govt. Prillt. Off., 2001. 73 p.

Legislative Action

Each of the minimum wage-related bills noted above has been referred to committee. None of them has as yet been enacted.

Chapter 4

OVERTIME PAY

A second component of the FLSA is its overtime pay requirement. Where workers are covered under the overtime pay provisions of the Act (Section 7), an employer must pay his employee 11/2 times the employee's *regular rate* (time-and-a-half) for hours worked in excess of a weekly standard-now, 40 hours. A range of exceptions has been built into the Act responding both to economics and to public policy concerns.

When considering the overtime pay requirements of the: Act, several elements "ought to be kept in mind. *First.* There is no daily limitation, under the FLSA, upon the number of hours that can be worked by an employee: just a weekly standard.[1] *Second.* There is no legal cap on the number of hours a person can work within a week so long as the worker is paid on a time-and-a-half basis for those hours worked in excess of 40 per week. *Third.* The Act allows flexibility. Within the context of a 40-hour workweek, any daily arrangement of work hours is permitted: i.e., 5 days of 8 hours each, 4 days of 10 hours each, 2 days of 20 hours each, etc. The option of employing workers on flexible and/or compressed schedules rests with the employer. Similarly, the decision to employ individuals on a more rigid fixed schedule of 40 hours with overtime pay at time-and-a-half is also an employer decision.[2]

---

1 In some cases, for reasons of public health and safety, shirt duration limits may be imposed, but these are not part of the FLSA

2 State laws may (and often do) provide somewhat different standards. Further, higher wage and hour (overtime pay) standards may result from collective bargaining agreements. However, the requirements of the FLSA *may not be reduced*-through collective bargaining.

In most sessions of Congress since 1938, proposals have been introduced that Would have modified the FLSA's overtime pay standards. The 107th Congress has been no exception.

STRUCTURING WORK HOURS REGULATION

Through the years, the contest for shorter hours of work has passed through a series of stages with shilling motivational emphases. During the 19th and early 20th centuries, various worker/trade union/reform groups campaigned first for the 10-hour workday and then for an 8-hour workday.[3] These demands were voiced largely (though by no means exclusively) in humane terms. Extended hours of work were deemed hazardous to an employee's physical and moral health, depriving him (or her) of opportunities for education, proper rearing of children, and participation in the democratic process. Excessively long hours of work in factories, mines, and fields, it was argued, left workers broken in health and spirit-and, by extension, similarly affected succeeding generations.[4] Following World War I and, increasingly, during the Great Depression, the impetus for reduced hours of work seemed to shirt. While social and humane consideration continued to be emphasized by trade unionists and reformers, economic considerations took on greater weight. High levels of Depression-era unemployment made some measure of work sharing, achieved through restraints upon the hours of work (e.g., over time pay requirements), seem more desirable. Various legislative initiatives-daily hours restrictions, a 30-hour workweek, etc.-were urged until, in 1938, Congress adopted the Fair Labor Standards Act. Under the FLSA, Congress dropped the concept of daily hours restraints and opted, instead, for what would become a 40-hour standard workweek with over time pay for hours worked in excess of 40 hours per week by covered workers.[5] By the end of World War II, the 40-

---

3 For a general overview, see Cahill, Marion C. *Shorter Hours: A Study of the Movement Since the Civil War.* New York, Columbia University Press, 1932.

4 The rationale for work hours regulation is explained in: Shorter Hours for Men as a Public Welfare Measure, *Monthly Labor Review,* June 1916, p. 23-29. Organized labor's approach to work hours reduction is explained in: McNeill, George. *The Eight Hour Primer", The Fact, Theory and the Argument.* Washington, American Federation of Labor, 1899; and in Gompers, Samuel. *The Eight Hour Workday: Its Inauguration, Enforcement and Influences.* Washington, American Federation of Labor, undated but published in pamphlet form at the turn of the century.

5 Concerning this period, see: Brandeis, Elizabeth. Organized Labor and Protective Labor Legislation, in Milton Derber and Edwin Young (eds.), *Labor and the New Deal.* Madison, The University of Wisconsin Press, 1961. p. 193-237.

hour workweek bad largely become the norm. Periodically, organized labor suggested further reduction, but no change was effected. In the late 1970s, a final campaign for a shorter workweek was initiated; but, following 3 days of hearings by the House Subcommittee on Labor Standards in 1979, the campaign gradually ended.[6]

With the passage of time, fewer persons were employed who bad directly experienced the economic turmoil of the Great Depression. For younger workers, the wage/hour protections afforded by the FLSA came increasingly to be taken as *a given:* they had become standard and accepted practice. The demographics of the workforce bad changed. More workers were better educated-and women had begun to have enhanced workforce attachment. By the 1960s, a new movement bad been commenced for *humanization* of the world-of-work and for flexibility.[7] In legislative form, the initiative was two-fold: alternative work scheduling for federal empl0yees and work hours flexibility for employees of state and 10cal governments. In the private sector, a significant number of employers instituted flexible and. compressed scheduling-both as a benefit for their employees and because it seemed a useful tool for structuring work.

In 1978, Congress passed legislation that provided for increasing part-time work opportunities in the federal sector (an option thought to be favored by working mothers) and, separately, allowed flexible and "compressed" work hours in federal agencies. These measures permitted a wide variation in work hours structuring and flexibility-but they did so within the context of federal civil service law and under the general oversight of the Congress.[8]

Since 1966, state and local government employees bad gradually been brought under the FLSA, but these extensions of coverage bad been litigated and it was not until the Supreme Court's decision in *Garcia v. San Antonio Metropolitan Transit Authority* (469 U.S. 528 (1985)) that the issue was decided. Like some private sector employers, state and local governments bad resisted coverage and bad argued that if the statute were applied without modification, the public agencies (and, by extension, the public)' would suffer financially. Thus, in late 1985 after the *Garcia* decision, Congress

---

6 See Fink, Gary (ed.). *AFL-CIG Executive Council Statements and Reports,* 1956-1975. Westport, Conn., Greenwood Press, 1977, p. 768, 986-988; and Ehrenberg, Ronald G., and Paul L. Schumann. *Longer Hours or More Jobs? An Investigation of Amending Hours Legislation To Create Employment.* Ithaca, Cornell University Press, 1982.

7 Among the earlier studies of workforce change in the 1960s and later were Poor, Riva. *4 Days, 40 Hours: Reporting a Revolution in Work and Leisure.* Cambridge, Bursk and Poor Publishing, 1970; and Sheppard, Harold L., and Neal Q" Herrick. *Where Have All the Robots Gone? Worker Dissatisfaction in the '70s.* New York, The Free Press, 1972.

8 P.L. *95-390* and P .L. 95-437. Legislation was necessary, in part, to set aside prior federal 8-hour daily limitations as they affected direct federal employees.

adopted special legislation allowing state and local government employers to utilize a "comp time" option. Congress also set forth detailed conditions under which the option might be implemented. As in the case of federal workers, the implementing agencies were normally permanent entities, were governed by civil service regulations, and were under general oversight of a legislative body.[9]

Some viewed the movement for alternative work scheduling as an erosion of labor standards that bad been developed through years of bargaining and legislative effort. Others, however, argued that the changing character of work and of the workforce bad rendered the wage/hour laws of the 1930s obsolete: the requirements of 1930s legislation should no longer be regarded as inviolate. *Flexibility* became the new by-word. And, almost immediate ly, the question was raised: If flexibility is appropriate for federal and state and local public employees, why not extend it to workers in the private sector?[10]

In the context of the FLSA, overtime pay requirements were viewed by Congress *as a penalty* that imposed a cost upon employers in order to encourage them not to schedule work hours in excess of 40 per week. The requirement or penalty was not intended as a mechanism through which to raise the wages of workers-through it may have bad that effect where employers have found it more convenient (and cheaper) to pay time-and-a-half rather than to hire additional workers. For some workers who are able, conveniently, to work more than 40 hours a week, overtime pay may be economically advantageous. For others whose personal lives may be less flexible (parents with small children, persons responsible for eldercare, students with rigid academic schedules, etc.), extended hours of work, even with extra pay, may not be welcome. Further, some may simply value free time more highly than additional income. And, some argue, extended hours, even in modem work environments, may increase the risk of accident or work-related impairment-endangering clients and the public.

Through the years, many employers have opposed overtime pay requirements. The cast factor is one obvious reason. Absent an overtime pay requirement, employers are able to engage workers through any number of

---

[9] P.L. *99-150.* See also CRS Report *96-570, Federal Regulations Of Working Hours: An* Overview Through the 105111 Congress, by William G. Whittaker.

[10] Some have argued that public and private work environments are essentially different. The former are stable, for the most part, and employees work within the context of civil service rules and under legislative oversight. In the private sector, employer/employee relations are diverse. In some cases, employmen l is stable, work patterns carefully structured, and trade union influence is strong. But, in others, employee turn over may be high, employers may easily move in and out of business, and the general context may be determinedly non-union.

hours at straight time. Further, as compensation has come increasingly to take the form of fringe benefits, even the payment of overtime rates may be cheaper than hiring additional workers. Thus, some have argued, an increase in the overtime rate to double time or higher may now be required if the penalty is to be effective. Additionally, employers have been concerned with control of their establishments. Work scheduling, traditionally, has been viewed as an employer prerogative: legislated wage/hour requirements, as an intrusion upon employer rights. Speaking generally (and with many exceptions), employers and employees have been split on the issue of overtime pay regulation. Workers have often urged an expansion of coverage and a strengthening of protections. Employers, on the other hand, have often called for less public restraint upon their *right to manage* and to run their business as they deem best-allowing them the opportunity to maximize profit.

LEGISLATION IN THE 107TH CONGRESS

Through several Congresses, employer interests have sought to *modernize* wage/hour laws that they regard as out-of-date and inconsistent with operation of the modern workplace.[11] At the same time, organized labor has tended to view such initiatives as an assault on fair labor standards. That campaign, with sharp dissents pro and con, has continued into the 107th Congress.

Exemption for the Funeral Industry

One method of exempting workers from the minimum wage under the FLSA and, more importantly, overtime pay requirements has been to treat certain employees as *executive, administrative, or professional workers*. That option is standard under Section 13(a)(1) of the Act. However, DOL

---

[11] Taking the lead in this initiative hag been the industry-oriented Labor Policy Association. Under date of October 7, 1994, the LP A issued a report, *Reinventing the Fair Labor Standards Act To Support the Reengineered Workplace.* It charged that "[i]n the archives of federal labor laws, the FLSA holds a position nearly comparable to that of the Dead Sea Scrolls" and stated: "... the FLSA's coverage rules have become so encrusted with meaningless distinctions that no employer can be completely confident which types of employees come within the Act's ambit." See V.S. Congress. House. Committee on Economic and Educational Opportunities, Subcommittee on Workforce Protections. *Hearings on the Fair Labor Standards Act.* Hearings, 104th Cong., 1st Sess., March 30, June 8, October 25, and November 1, 1995. Washington, U.S. Govt. Print Off., 1996. p. 26.

has been concerned that workers not be arbitrarily labeled as *executive, administrative, or professional* by employers seeking to circumvent legitimate FLSA wage/hour requirements.

In attempting to distinguish a professional person from a worker who is technically trained and highly skilled, the Department established certain criteria of assessment. For example, the work of a professional must require:

> ...knowledge of an advance[d] type in a field of science or learning customarily acquired by a prolonged course of specialized intellectual instruction and study, as distinguished from a general academic education and from an apprenticeship, and from training in the performance of routine mental, manual, or physical processes ...

DOL has emphasized the "original and creative character" of such work and the "exercise of discretion and judgment" in its performance. It must be predominantly what the worker actually does: i.e., the major portion of his or her work. And, the worker must be paid at a professional's rate.[12]

The funeral industry sought Section 13(a)(1) professional exemption for certain of its workers and, when DOL demurred, Senator Lauch Faircloth (R-N.C.) introduced legislation in the 105th Congress that would have exempted, by statute, licensed funeral directors (not owners of mortuaries but, rather, employees) from FLSA wage/hour protection. The Senator pointed to "the economic hardship" and "financial strain" such requirements place on small business owners who have "to allocate revenues for that purpose"-ie., paying their employees at least the minimum wage and overtime pay for hours worked in excess of 40 per week.[13] No action was taken on the Faircloth proposal; but, the issue resurfaced in the 106th Congress and was expanded to exempt both licensed funeral directors and licensed embalmers. The initiative became enmeshed within the general minimum wage debate and died at the close of the 106th Congress.

In the 107th Congress, Representative Graham has reintroduced the issue (H.R. 648). A comparable provision is included in H.R. 546 (Quinn).[14]

---

[12] See 29 CFR 541.3(a) forward. For a detailed discussion of this issue, see CRS Report *RL30697, FuneralServices: The Industry, its Workforce, and Labor Standards,* by William G. Whittaker.

[13] *Congressional Record* (daily edition), July 31,1998, p. 89562.

[14] H.R. 3678 (Graham) would similarly amend the FLSA to exempt from minimum wage and overtime pay requirements "certain construction engineering and design professionals" as defined in the proposed legislation.

Computer Services Professionals

During the 1980s, the computer industry sought to classify certain of it employees as *professionals* under Section 13(a)(1) of the FLSA-eliminating their regular minimum wage and overtime pay protections. As in the case of the funeral industry, the definition of *professional* presented a problem. In the rapidly evolving computer technology field, marked by fluctuating educational standards and often ill-defined responsibilities, the Department found it difficult to determine who was a *professional* for purposes of FLSA exemption and who was just a very highly skilled technician.

During consideration of the 1989 FLSA amendments, language was proposed that would have allowed wage/hour exemption (special treatment) of certain computer services workers *as professionals,*[15] The initial minimum wage legislation (to which the computer services exemption bad been appended) was vetoed by President Bush and, when a subsequent measure was passed and signed, the computer services exemption bad been dropped. The following year, however, the exemption, combined with another unrelated amendment to the FLSA, was passed and signed (P .L. 101-583).[16] The amendment included a requirement-with respect to this group of workers only-that conditioned exemption upon payment of an hourly wage equal to "at least 6½ times" the applicable minimum wage under the FLSA.

In 1996, the issue was revisited. New FLSA/minimum wage amendments were taken up as a floor amendment to tax legislation reported from the Committee on Ways and Means. There bad been no hearing on the computer services exemption and the provision sparked little floor discussion. The restructured exemption (P .L. 104-188) added a new paragraph (17) to Section 13(a). Thus, the new language circumvented the issue of *professional* status in Paragraph (1) of Section 13(a), establishing a specific categorical exemption for the specified computer services workers. The "6½ times" formula earnings test was abandoned and replaced with an equivalent flat rate of $27.63 an hour: i.e., 6½ times the applicable minimum wage *at that time*. The 1996 language also defined which workers (by job description) were to be eligible for exemption.

In the 106th Congress, a proposal to amend and broaden the computer services exemption was introduced-both as a free-standing bill and as part of general FLSA/minimum wage legislation. While the fixed dollar volume threshold was retained ($27.63), its value would have dropped to 5.4 times

---

[15] *Congressional Record* (daily edition), Apri l12, 1989, p. *S3741.*

[16] *Congressional Record* (daily edition), October 18, 1990, p. H10563-H10565, and October 27, 1990, *S.17679.*

the minimum wage. However, both the computer services proposal and the minimum wage legislation died at the close of the 106th Congress. In the 107th Congress, two bills expanding the computer service worker exemption were early introduced: B.R. 546 (Quinn), a general umbrella proposal dealing largely with non-FLSA issues but expanding the computer service worker provision of the FLSA as well; and B.R. 1545 (Andrews), free-standing legislation dealing with wage/hour treatment of computer services personnel.[17]

Inside Sales Workers

From the 103rd through the 106th Congresses, legislation was introduced that would have exempted from FLSA minimum wage and overtime pay requirements employers of certain "inside sales" workers. These proposals were not enacted.[18] In 1938, Congress provided an exemption from FLSA minimum wage and overtime pay protection for certain persons employed "in the capacity of outside salesman" (now Section 13(a)(1) of the Act). Such persons, working beyond their employer's base of operations, were difficult to monitor in terms of hours worked while a precise ratio of hours to wages for minimum wage calculation was almost impossible to achieve. Thus, an exemption was deemed necessary. Subsequently, special treatment was afforded certain retail and service workers paid on a commission basis and meeting other qualifications (Section 7(i)).

At least by the early 1990s, concern was voiced with respect to the relative competitive positions of wholesale and retail firms (treated differently under the Act) and of "inside" and "outside" sales staff. Outside sales personnel, some argued, bad greater flexibility in that they could visit with clients in person during hours that made sense to the latter; whereas, inside sales people were desk or counter bound and worked on more or less fixed schedules. It would be an expansion of *opportunity,* it was argued, to free "inside" sales staff from FLSA restrictions, allowing them to work longer hours (without an overtime pay constraint) and, thereby, to earn more. Thus, it was proposed that distinctions between "inside" and "outside" sales staff be modified. The change would make the law more equitable, proponents argued.

---

[17] See CRS Report RI30537, *Computer Services Personnel: Overtime Pay Under the Fair Labor Standards Act,* by William G. Whittaker.

[18] See CRS Report RL30003, *Modi.fying Minimum Wage and Overtilne Pay Coverage for Certain Sales Employees under the Fair Labor Standards Act,* by William G. Whittaker.

Critics of the proposal suggested that the projected amendment was unjustified: that it would leave without FLSA minimum wage and overtime pay protection workers who were previously *covered inside* sales personnel. It was not clear, they stated, that elimination of wage/hour protections would make inside sales personnel any more efficient or expand their capacity to sell. Rather, critics contended, the measure may merely provide an opportunity for employers to circumvent the minimum wage and overtime pay requirements of current law while shifting any additional costs of selling (time and effort) from the employer to the worker. Besides, it was argued, employees were free to work flexible hours under current law without overtime pay constraints-assuming that their employers were willing to have them do so.

In the 107th Congress, the issue has resurfaced in H.R. 546 (Quinn), an umbrella bill that deals with wage/hour treatment for "inside sales" workers but with other matters as well. Free-standing legislation, H.R. 2070 (Tiberi), dealing with the proposed inside sales exemption was introduced June 6, 2001. A general oversight hearing on the inside sales exemption issue was conducted by the House Subcommittee on Workforce Protections on June 7, 2001. While employer spokespersons supported the proposed "inside sales" exemption, a trade union witness spoke against it. Other comment was mixed.

On June 27, the Subcommittee conducted a mark-up session on H.R. 2070. Representative Owens, although opposed to the legislation, urged that the threshold for exemption be increased to retain wage/hour protection for low-wage sales workers.[19] Representative Woolsey, also in opposition, called for worker *choice*-urging that the decision to work overtime hours without wage/hour protection (but with the potential for enhanced sales commissions) be made "voluntary" on the part of the worker. The Owens and Woolsey amendments were voted down and the bill was approved and ordered to be reported to the full Committee on Education and the Workforce. The votes were slang party lines: Republicans in favor of an "inside sales" exemption; Democrats, in opposition.[20]

---

19 Under H.R. 2070, the exemption threshold would be $22,500. Representative Owens proposed raising it to 6½ times the current minimum wage (i.e., $69,618.), a rate that he stated would more nearly reflect a professional status. (See discussion of the computer services exemption, above.) Representative Isakson, viewing the exemption as an option favorable to workers, argued that the higher threshold would unfairly limit sales opportunities for beginning workers.

20 Bureau of National Affairs. *Daily Labor Report*, June 28, 2001, p. AA1.

Restructuring Overtime Flexibility for Private Sector Employers

Since the mid-1980s, various initiatives have been introduced that would have restructured the overtime pay requirements of the FLSA to permit (but not require) private sector employers to offer their workers a "comp time" option in lieu of overtime pay for hours worked in excess of a statutory standard. Proposals varied. Some bills called for restructuring the "workweek" into more extended units: i.e., 2 week (80 hour) or 4 week (160 hour) periods. Some versions of the legislation proposed a system of "flexible credit hours" and the systematic banking of overtime hours through extended periods. Other variations were also suggested, shifting from one bill to another.

An argument central to debate on the issue of restructuring hours of work has been the question of FLSA flexibility. Diversity in the workplace was anticipated by Congress in shaping federal wage/hour legislation and, therefore, it built some measure of flexibility into the FLSA. At present, employers are permitted, with no overtime pay penalty, to structure weekly work hours in any configuration of their choice. They can allow workers flexible arrival and departure times and "comp time" in which work hours can migrate from one day to another. The workweek, itself, can be structured as a routine period of 5 days of 8 horns each or, at the employer's discretion, it can be recompressed info 4 days of 10 hours each, 2 days of 20 hours each, or any other arrangement not exceeding 40 hours within a 7-day period.[21] However, flexibility, under most proposals, would have remained an employer option -or, where there is a collective bargaining agreement in place, with workers and employers jointly.

Hearings on the various proposals were technical and contentious. Proponents, largely (but not entirely) ignoring employer interest in restructuring the workweek, argued for more flexibility for workers-especially for "soccer moms." They stressed that a 1930s statute (the FLSA) stood in the way of creation of a *family friendly* workplace. Critics argued that the Act already contained flexibility if employers choose to utilize it. The proposed legislation, they contended would provide *employer flexibility* and not *worker flexibility.* With creative scheduling by employers, they argued, overtime protection could become a deal letter.

---

[21] More extended workweeks are permitted, of course, but work hours in excess of 40 per week must be compensated at *time-and-a-half* rate.

As reflected in the hearings and debates through several Congresses, the issues seemed to come down to three issues. *First.* Were these proposals actually concerned with work hours fallibility for *workers* or were they a disguised attempt by employers to abrogate existing labor standards? *Second.* Assuming that the concern with flexibility for workers was genuine, were sufficient safeguards included within the proposals so that flexibility would not be abused? *Third.* Would the flexibility proposals present any special problems for the DOL (or for employers) in terms of their implementation or for enforcement and compliance?

Through several years, the proposals were modified with safeguards being added to counter labor's concerns. But, ultimately, lines pro and con seem to have been sharply drawn: employer interests in support of the work hours fallibility legislation; labor, strongly opposed. Individuals argued on each side of the issue.[22]

In the 107th Congress, new legislation (S. 624) has been introduced by Senator Gregg. The bill would allow an employer to provide "compensatory time off" to employees in lieu of overtime. And, it would allow compressed scheduling through a bi-weekly work period, substituting an 80-hour work period for the standard 40-horn workweek with the caveat "that no more than10 hours may be shifted between the 2 weeks involved." The bill contains other provisions as well. H.R. 1982, introduced by Representative Biggert, is a single-purpose proposal authorizing the use of compensatory time off for employees of private sector employers.

Clarifying the Concept of *Regular Rate*

Under the FLSA, a covered worker engaged through more than 40 hours in a single workweek, must be compensated for hours worked in excess of 40 "at a rate of not less than one and one- half times the regular rate" at which he is paid: i.e., *time-and-a-half.* Although the concept of *regular rate* is set forth in Section 7(e) of the Act, questions have continued to arise. For example, under Section 7(e), the *regular rate* "shall be deemed to include all remuneration for employment paid to, or on behalf of, the employee." But, then, perhaps, not quite an; for there follows within Section 7(e) seven paragraphs enumerating what the *regular rate "shall not be deemed to*

[22] See CRS Report 96-570, *Federal Regulation of Working Hours: An Overview Through the 105th Congress, by* William G. Whittaker; and CRS Report 97-532, *Federal Regulation of Working Hours: Consideration of the Issues Through the 105th Congress*, by William G.

include." (Italics added.) These exceptions include, but are not limited to, such things as "sums paid as gifts," "payments made for occasional periods when no work is performed due to vacation, holiday, illness," etc. The inventory is extensive but it still leaves open an opportunity for confusion with respect to the specific definition of *regular rate.*[23]

In the 106th Congress, Representative Ballenger sought to clarify the issue by expanding the inventory of elements not to be included within the concept of *regular rate.* The Subcommittee on Workforce Protections conducted hearings on the Ballenger proposal. Although marked-up and reported from the full Committee on Education and the Workforce, the bill was not called up for floor consideration.[24] Meanwhile, a House-passed bankruptcy reform bill was moving through the Senate and the substance of the Ballenger proposal was added to it in the Senate-and passed. Before a conference report on the bankruptcy legislation could be agreed upon, Congress adjourned.

On April 26, 2001, Representative Ballenger introduced new legislation (H.R. 1602) on the "regular rate" issue. It would add to the list of elements *not to be included* in calculation of the regular rate any payments:

> ...made to reward an employee or group of employees for meeting or exceeding the productivity, quality, efficiency, or sales goals as specified in a gain sharing plan, incentive bonus plan, commission plan, or performance contingent bonus plan ...

Speaking broadly, the legislation has been supported by industry and opposed by spokespersons for labor. The latter expressed concern than regular wage rates could be reduced with greater emphasis (and reward) assigned to various incentive programs. The option could also be used, some felt, to encourage an unjustified "speed-up" in production processes that would lead to increased potential for accidents and, with time, to reduced earnings.

Whittaker. The first is an historical overview; the latter, a summation of hearings and debates.

23 Concerning a closely related issue, see CRS Report RL30542, *Stock Options and Overtime Pay Calculation Under the Fair Labor Standards Act,* by William G. Whittaker.

24 U.S. Congress. House. Committee on Education and the Workforce. *Rewarding Performance in Compensation Act, Report Together with Minority Views To Accompany H.R.1381.* H.Rept.106-358, 106th Cong., 1st Sess. Washington, Govt. Print. Off., October 1, 1999. 24 p. Companion legislation (S. 1878) was introduced by Senator Hutchison of Texas, but was not acted upon.

In part, it appears, to respond to such concerns, Representative Ballenger added the following safeguards to the bill. To qualify under the terms of H.R. 1602, a plan:

> ...shall be in writing and made available to employees, provide that the amount of the payments to be made under the plan be based upon a formula that is stated in the plan, and be established and maintained in good faith for the purpose of distributing to employees additional remuneration over and above the wages and salaries that are not dependent upon the existence of such plan or payments made pursuant to such plan.

Mr. Ballenger explained: "Predominance bonuses and gain sharing programs are a way for employees to share in the success of the company they work for."[25]

A Workforce Protections Subcommittee hearing on July 31, 2001 displayed sharp divisions with respect to H.R. 1602. Employer spokespersons and other proponents of the legislation spoke in terms of rewarding workers. Representative Biggert affirmed that H.R. 1602 "will encourage employers to reward their employees and make it easier for employers to 'share the wealth'..."[26] Leonard Court of the U .S. Chamber of Commerce spoke in terms of "productivity, efficiency or incentive," suggesting that workers could be encouraged to "give maximum effort" through a system of bonuses or gain sharing. "[W]e know," he stated, "that financial incentives motivate workers to better performance." Many employers, he added, "believe that performance-based incentives are the most productive war to motivate and reward at both the individual and group levels." They would also make companies "more competitive" while employees would have "predictable rewards for achieving specified goals."[27]

The industry-oriented Labor Policy Association (LP A), which endorsed H.R. 1602, presented a somewhat different perspective. lncentive plans, it affirmed, "have been around almost since the industrial age first began." An employee might earn a bonus if he (or she) worked "more quickly than the time the employer bad allotted for the task The quicker the employee worked, the faster his or her pay increased over the base rate for the job." Today's incentive plans, the LP A noted, "are significantly different." It explained: "These pro grams are focused on achieving important ; business goals When the goals are reached," LPA stated, "the employees receive " a financial bonus, which is usually part of the amounts the company saved by

25 *Congressional Record,* April 26, 2001, p. E642.

26 Statement of Representative Judy Biggert, July 31, 2001.

27 Statement of Leonard Court, July 31, 2001.

c. achieving the business goals." It dubbed bonus and gain sharing plans "a will-will proposition for employees and employers because they increase employee pay while improving productivity and workplace relations."[28]

Others dissented. While "employers would generally still have to pay the minimum wage," the legislation would encourage them "to convert all additional compensation into bonuses," protested Representative Owens. Overtime pay (the *regular rate)* would be calculated on the basis of the base rate; any bonus income would be outside of that calculation. Thus, he suggested, the employer could pay lower wages and enjoy a reduced rate when workers were asked to work overtime hours. H.R. 1602, he argued, could lead to wage rate manipulation and undermining of the overtime pay requirements of the Act -neither to the advantage of the worker.[29]

Michael Leibig, representing the AFL-CIO, concurred with Representative Owens. He pointed to five major objections to H.R. 1602. *First,* it would "fundamentally undermine the FLSA and its encouragement of the 40 hour work week." *Second,* it would "reduce the take home pay of hundreds of thousands" of workers. *Third,* it would "reduce the compensation of all Americans who work overtime hours." *Fourth,* it would "encourage the present lengthening" of the workweek and "lead to additional forced overtime." *Fifth,* it would shift the pay structure to increase the proportion of income from bonuses while reducing the level of regular wages. Then, Leibig added that the legislation was simply unnecessary. Bonus and gainsharing plans "flourish" under current law, he averred: "Those systems exists [sic] and are spreading under the current requirements of the Fair Labor Standards Act. There is nothing in the Act which impedes or prevents this."[30]

In interviews following the hearing, industry spokespersons indicated no disposition to make further modifications in the language of the bill to meet labor's objections. But, then, critics of the legislation remained firm in their position. "I have never been persuaded that there is a need for H.R. 1602," Representative Owens concluded. "Employers were paying bonuses before the Fair Labor Standards Act was enacted and continue to now."[31]

---

28 Statement of the Labor Policy Association, July 31, 2001. Some might argue that this would .encourage a "speed-up" of the production process with the *goal,* set by management, ever more distant and elusive.

29 Statement of Representative Major Owens, July 31, 2001.

30 Statement of Michael Leibig, July 31, 2001. Others would dispute that contention, arguing that lifting bureaucratic requirements would significantly expand such options.

31 Bureau of National Affairs, *Daily Labor Report,* August 1, 2001. p. AA1-AA2.

Prohibiting *Forced* Overtime Work for Licensed Health Care Employees

Regulation of work hours, as noted above, has several purposes: humane consideration with respect to individual workers, the economic concern with sharing the available work, and public safety. Frequently, these several element can combine in a single initiative. Overtime work required of healthcare professionals is such a case.

On May 30, 2001, in response to concerns that excessive hours of work may be detriment al to health care workers *and* endanger their patients, Representative Lantos introduced B.R. 1289. If enacted, the bill would prevent an employer from *requiring* "a licensed health care employee (including a registered nurse but not including a physician) to work more than 8 hours in any workday or 80 hours in any 14-day work period, except in the case of a natural disaster" or during a "state of emergency" in the locality.[32] An employer would not be allowed to "discriminate or take any other adverse action against such an employee for declining to work more than 8 hours in a workday or 80 hours in a 14-day work period." However: "Such an employee may voluntarily work more than 8 hours a day or more then 80 hours in a 14-day work period." A similar (but not identical) bill (B.R. 1902) was introduced on July 20, 2001, by Representative Langevin. Each bill, providing for amendment of the FLSA, was referred to the Committee on Education and the Workforce.7S[33]

As further information began to surface, additional measures were proposed. On November 5, 2001, Representative Stark introduced H.R. 3238, the "Safe Nursing and Patient Care Act of 2001." Branding mandatory overtime as "a very real quality of care issue for our health system," the Congressman observed:

> We have existing government standards that limit the hours that pilots, flight attendants, truck drivers, railroad engineers, and other professionals can safety work before consumer safety could be impinged. However, no similar limitation currently exists for OUT nation's nurses who are caring for us at often the most vulnerable times in our lives.[34]

---

32 Under Section *7G)* of the FLSA, certain employees of healthcare institutions are allowed to work a 14-day bi-weekly period rather than the otherwise standard 40 hour workweek. The Lantos bill, it is argued, would strengthen worker protections of current law.

33 On June 13, 2001, Governor Angus King of Maine signed into law a measure restricting mandatory overtime for nurses except in "unforeseen emergency circumstances when overtime is required as a last resort to ensure patient safety ." Bureau of National Affairs. *Daily Labor Report,* June 18, 2001. p. A8.

34 *Congressional Record,* November 6, 2001, p. E2007.

On November 14, 2001, companion legislation (8.1686) was introduced by Senator Kennedy. "Job dissatisfaction and overtime hours are major factors in the current shortage of nurses," the Senator stated. He added, "Improving conditions for nurses-is an essential part of our ongoing effort to reduce medical errors, improve patient outcomes, and encourage more Americans to become and remain nurses."[35] Acknowledging that the "hospital trade associations" may not applaud the legislation, Representative Stark noted that it had won the endorsement of the American Nurses Association and other worker-oriented groups.[36]

On July 17, 2001, Senator Rockefeller introduced S. 1188, the "Department of Veterans Affairs Medical Programs Enhancement Act of 2001." (A proposal with siillilar provisions was introduced by Representative Udall (N.Mex.) on October 3, 2001 -H.R. 3017.) The legislation followed in the wake of a June 14, 2001, hearing by the Committee on Veterans' Affairs, Senator Rockefeller explained, which bad focused upon "the imminent shortage of professional nurses." After discussing the content of the legislation, the Senator concluded, "We must encourage higher enrollment in nursing schools, improve the work environment, and offer nurses opportunities to develop as respected professionals, while taking steps to ensure safe staffing levels in the short-term."[37] On October 10, 2001, S. 1188 was reported favorably from the Committee on Veterans' Affairs.[38]

---

[35] *Congressional Record,* November 14, 2001, p. S11794.

[36] *Congressional Record,* November 6, 2001, p. E2007.

[37] *Congressional Record,* July 17, 2001, p. S7819.

[38] U.S. Congress. Senate. Committee on Veterans' Affairs. *Department of Veterans Affairs Medical Programs Enhancement Act 012001, Report to Accompany S.* 1188. S .Rept. 107-80, 107th Cong., 1st Sess. Washington, Govt. Print. Off., October 10,2001.

Chapter 5

CHILD LABOR

During the past 2 decades, intermittent legislative interest has focused upon the problem of child labor. At large, the issue can be divided into two general spheres: practices within the United States and those in foreign countries. Although the core issue (the treatment of children who work) may be the same in each case, the areas are approached somewhat differently. Domestic American child labor is regulated under the FLSA In a global context, child labor is beyond the scope of the FLSA (and of this report) and more nearly a subject for trade legislation and of international human fights accords.[1]

CHILD LABOR IN THE UNITED STATES

Concern about child labor in the United States can be divided, roughly, into four periods. *First.* From the late 19th century to 1941, reformers sought to remove children from the workplace (whether factory, field, or tenement house) and to make school attendance mandatory. *Second.* With World War II, the focus shifted to alleged labor shortages for war production. Some urged modification of work restrictions for older children (too young for the draft but old enough to be useful employees) and an easing of school attendance requirements. *Third.* By the late 1940s, another shift bad taken

---

1 See CRS Report RS20445, *Child Labor and the International Labor Organization (ILO)*, by Lois McHugh. In April 2001, for example, the DOL announced that it would provide $4.3 million to the ILO "for a program to combat child labor trafficking in West and Central Africa." Bureau of National Affairs, *Daily Labor Report*, April 24, 2001, p. A3-A4. In the 107th Congress, bills dealing in some measure with child labor in a global setting include H.R. 473 (Rivers), H.R. 627 (Boehner), and S. 333 (Lugar).

place. Too many older youths were believed to be out-of-school, out-of-work, and unable to find employment for which, it was argued, they were often unprepared both in terms of training and discipline. Thus, various "school- to-work transition" programs were developed and" concern shifted from oppressive child labor to excessive youth joblessness. *Fourth.* Very largely, after the early 1940s, most perhaps assumed that the *problem* of oppressive child labor bad been relegated to the realm of history. Then, in 1982, the Reagan Administration proposed a general revision of federal child labor regulation.[2] That proposal, never promulgated in final form, sparked controversy and appears to have reignited concern about the conditions under which young Americans are employed. Concern about child labor regulation continues, however, with proposals reflecting a variety of perspectives.

LEGISLATIVE PROPOSALS OF THE 107TH CONGRESS

Since the early 1980s, child labor has been the subject of numerous hearings. Bach session of the Congress has seen new legislation submitted: sometimes further to restrict the employment of children; at other times, to broaden their opportunities for employment. Several child labor bills have now been introduced in the 107th Congress.

Young American Workers' Bill of Rights

On March 8, 2001, Representative Lantos introduced B.R. 961, the "Young American Workers' Bill of Rights."

The Lantos bill is comprehensive. (a) It requires the Secretary of Labor and the United States Census Bureau to compile data on the extent and nature of child labor in America, including an inventory of work-related injuries or illnesses involving child workers. (b) It redefines "minor" to include "an individual who is under. the age of 18 and who has not received a high school diploma or its equivalent or who is 18 and enrolled full-time in a high school." Such minors may not be employed in the absence of "a valid certificate of employment" issued by "a State agency." It sets forth in detail

[2] In general, the Reagan Administration proposals would have relaxed restrictions upon employment of children. See: U.S. Congress. House of Representatives. Committee on Education and Labor, Subcommittee on Labor Standards. Hearings. *Oversight Hearings-*

the conditions to be satisfied, prior to issuance of such certificates of employability. (c) It directs the Secretary of Labor to revise the existing system of hazardous occupation orders (HO's), listing types of work unsuitable by reason of their hazardous character for persons under a specified age. (d) It revises the penalty structure for child labor violators-both for criminal and civil penalties. (e) It mandates "closer working relationships among Federal and State agencies having responsibility for enforcing labor, safety and health, and immigration laws." (f) It affirms that: "The Secretary of Labor shall publish and disseminate the names and addresses of each person who has willfully violated the provisions of Section 12 of the Fail Labor Standards Act of 1938 relating to child labor or any regulation under such section and the types of violations committed by such person and shall distribute the publication regionally." The names of employers who violate federal child labor law will be made "available to affected school districts." (g) It eliminates any .small business exemption from the amended statute. And (h), it defines as oppressive child labor employment of any person "under the age of 14 ...as a migrant agricultural worker ...or seasonal agricultural worker."[3]

Traveling Sales Crew Protection Act

In the mid-1980s, public attention was drawn to "unscrupulous door-to-door selling groups" who were alleged to be exploiting young persons (some, children; others, young adults). At the urging of then-Representative Wyden, hearings were conducted on the issue by the House Subcommittee on Civil and Constitutional Rights.[4] While DOL conceded that there was a problem, it professed no need for legislation *at that time.* Subsequent hearings were conducted by the Senate Permanent Subcommittee on Investigations (1987) and by the Subcommittee on Employment and Housing, House Committee on Government Operations (1990). Though Representative Lantos proposed legislation in the 103rd Congress that would have curtailed door-to-door sales by persons under 16 years of age, no further action was taken.

Proposed Changes in Child Labor Regulations. 97^th^C ong., 2nd Sess., Washington, V.S. Govt. Print. Off., 1982. 144 p.

3 For an explanation of current child labor regulation under the FLSA, see Title 29 CFR, Part 570 ff. AB in other areas of labor standards regulation, many states have laws dealing with children who are employed. In addition, unlike adult workers, child workers may be subject to school attendance laws.

4 *Congressional Record,* May 16, 1985 (daily edition), p. E2251.

In 1999, the issue again surfaced and Senator Kohl introduced legislation to curb/regulate youth participation in traveling sales work, but no action was taken on the Kohl bill Again, in the 107th Congress, Senator Kohl has introduced legislation in this area: S. 96, the "Traveling Sales Crew Protection Act." The Kohl bill would amend the FLSA to provide that "No individual under 18 years of age may be employed in a position requiring the individual to engage in door to door sales or in related support work in a manner that requires the individual to remain away from his or her permanent residence for more than 24 hours." After defining the operative language, the bill sets forth a registration requirement for employers and supervisors of traveling sales crew workers. Then, where such practices are allowed, it sets out the obligations of the parties-dealing with such items as housing, transportation, wages (and deductions the reform), insurance, etc. It then lays out a system for enforcement. (See also H.R. 3070 (Petri), introduced October 9, 2001.)

The *CARE* Act of 2001

In the 107th Congress, two bills have been introduced, each with the same title: the "Children's Act for Responsible Employment of 2001" or the "CARE Act." The bills are not identical.

The Harkin CARE Act

On May 10, 2001, Senator Harkin introduced S. 869, which was referred to the Committee on Health, Education, Labor, and Pensions. The Harkin Bill begins by focusing upon the employment of children in agriculture other than those who are employed by an immediate family member on a farm owned or operated by such family member. It then moves on to restructuring the civil and criminal penalties for child labor law violations at large. It directs the Secretary of Labor and the Director of the Bureau of the Census to compile, biannually, data concerning (a) the types of industries and occupations in which children under 18 years of age are employed and (b) cases in which children were employed in violation of FLSA child labor provisions. The bill would also require certain reports by employers of persons under 18 years of age. Finally, the Secretaries of Labor and Health and Human Services would be required to issue a biannual report on the status of child labor in the United States "and its attendant safety and health hazards." The bill would also delete certain portions of existing law, thus tightening protective labor standards.

The Roybal-Allard CARE ACT

On June 19, 2001, Representative Roybal-Allard introduced H.R. 2239, which was referred to the Committee on Education and the Workforce and to the Committee on Agriculture. With some variations in language, H.R. 2239 incorporates the substance of S. 869.

The Roybal-Allard bill, however, goes much further than the Harkin bill. *First.* H.R. 2239 calls for employment of "at least 100 additional inspectors within the Wage and Hour Division" of DOL "for the principal purpose of enforcing compliance with child labor laws." It also calls for a 10% increase in the budget of the Solicitor of Labor for prosecution of child labor law violations. *Second.* The federal Insecticide, Fungicide, and Rodenticide Act would be amended to direct that special standards with respect to pesticide use where children and pregnant or nursing women are present (near) or employed be developed. It would mandate a review of such standards every 5 years, promulgation of specific requirements for the conduct of pesticide-related inspections, and annual publication of the "findings and results of such inspections for each State." *Third.* The Workforce Investment Act of 1998 would be amended to provide a new "Migrant and Seasonal Farm worker Youth Dropout Prevention" pro gram designed to strengthen and expand educational and training opportunities for migratory youth.

To Protect Youth Workers from Social Harm

On May 16, 2001, Representative Frost introduced the "Amy Robinson Memorial Act," H.R. 1869, which would amend the FLSA by adding a new Section 14(e)(1).

H.R. 1869, designed to assure that a parent or guardian is given "prompt written notice" in cases in which a youth is employed in association with a fellow worker who has a history of violent crime. It directs the Secretary of Labor to provide such notice where (a) the employee is under 18 years of age or employed under DOL certification in a sheltered work environment, (b) the employer "knows or reasonably should know that the earning or productive capacity of the employee is impaired by physical or mental deficiency, or injury," (c) another individual with "a criminal record that includes a conviction for a crime of violence... performs work at the same facility as the employee," and (d) the employer "employs the other individual; or... knows or reasonably should know of the conviction." The notice to the parent or guardian of the youth or disabled worker "shall contain an identification of the facility, a statement that an individual who bad been convicted of a crime of violence performs work at the facility, and an identification of each such crime of violence."

In a news release, Representative Frost explained that Amy Robinson, late of Arlington, Texas, a "mentally challenged women ...was murdered by a co-worker in 1998." He stated that he was introducing the legislation (identical to a bill he had introduced in the 106th Congress) to ensure "that parents receive written notice if their child starts a new job where they will be working with a violent felon."[5]

Sawmill Work by 14 Year Olds

Work in or around sawmills and wood-working machinery has been deemed by DOL as especially hazardous for young persons under 18 years of age. The practice violates at least two DOL Hazardous Occupations Orders: HO 4, covering sawmills, and HO 5, dealing with power-driven wood working machines.[6]

The Amish of Pennsylvania (and of other states) resist requirements of law that would alter their traditional way of life. Many Amish avoid modern conveniences and have rejected compulsory school attendance beyond the 8th grade. The *Daily Labor Report* explains: "After completing their formal classroom training at age 14 or 15, Amish boys typically receive training in farming or carpentry from their fathers."[7] The declining opportunity to farm (in part, because of increased land values) have led the Amish to have their children work in sawmills and wood-working plants and, thus, to a clash with DOL over implementation of HO 4 and HO 5.

In the 105th and 106th Congresses, legislation was introduced both in the House and in the Senate that would, under specified conditions, have widened the opportunity for youth aged 14 years to 18 years "to be employed inside or outside places of business where machinery is used to process wood products." The bills were sponsored, respectively, by Representative Pitts and Senator Specter. One qualification would have been that the youth "is a member of a religious sect or division thereof whose established

---

5 Press release from the office of Representative Martin Front, May 17, 2001.

6 See 29 CFR 570.54 and 750.55. In a letter of July 22, 1998, to Chairman William F. Goodling, Chair of the Committee on Education and the Workforce, Deputy Secretary of Labor Kathryn Higgins explained the special hazards associated with work in the lumber and wood products industry which, she said, were "exacerbated for youth" given their "lack of training" and "immaturity."

7 Bureau of National Affairs, *Daily Labor Report,* July 23, 1998, p. All.

teachings do not permit formal education beyond the eighth grade." In each Congress, the Amish legislation was passed by the House under suspension; the Senate did not act in either case.[8]

In effect, were the legislation to be adopted, Amish children, having left school after the 8th grade, would be allowed to be employed in work otherwise regarded as too hazardous for persons under 18 years of age. Some have suggested constitutional issues might be raised by affording special treatment to members of one religious group that are not afforded to others. Setting aside issues of legality, several other questions could be raised in the context of the proposed legislation. *First.* Is it wise public policy to allow youngsters (even the Amish) to drop out of school after the 8th grade? *Second.* Does elimination of federal restrictions upon child labor (to the extent proposed in the legislation) provide an opportunity (and, perhaps, an incentive) for Amish children to leave school and to enter the world-of-work? *Third.* Assuming that these children do leave school to work, are sawmills/wood processing establishments appropriate places of employment for any youngsters under the age of 18 years?

In order to strengthen the ties of Amish children to the Amish community, they are systematically separated from the non-Amish world.[9] The work experience and skills which they are afforded *may not* be readily transferable to the non-Amish marketplace. Thus, with only an 8th grade education and lacking experience in the non-Amish world, the choices of Amish youth may, accordingly, be restricted, rendering their out-migration from the community within which they were raised extremely difficult. While some may applaud this result, others may question the appropriateness of the role of the federal government in its facilitation. Since Amish children are permitted to leave school at 14 years of age, their subsequent activity may become a federal policy issue. Should they be permitted/required to work and, if so, at what types of tasks? What types of work are suitable for such children—and who should decide? As directed under the current law, DOL has reviewed the conditions of work in sawmills and woodworking

---

8 *Congressional Record* (daily edition), September 28, 1998, H9121-H9124. See also: U.S. Congress. House. Committee on Education and the Workforce, Subcommittee on Workforce Protections. *The Effect of the Fair Labor Standards Act on Amish Families and HR. 2038, the MSPA Clarification Act.* Hearing, 105th Cong., 2nd Sess., April 21, 1998. Washington, U.S. Govt. Print. Off., 1998; and, V.S. Congress. House. Committee on Education and the Workforce. *Amending the Fair Labor Standards Act of* 1938 *To Permit Certain Youth To Perform Certain Work with Wood Products, Report Together with Minority Views To Accompany H.R.* 221. H.Rept.106-31, 106th Cong., 1st Sess. Washington, V.S. Govt. Print. Off., 1999. 29 p.

9 Brown, Jennifer. Old Ways Persevere, Flourish: Non-Mainstream Culture Helps Anabaptist Communities Retain Hold on the Young. *The Washington Post,* April 21, 2001, p.B9.

facilities and bad deemed such activity especially hazardous for any youth under 18 years of age.[10]

On May 3, 2001, the Senate Appropriations Committee, Subcommittee on Labor, Health and Human Services, and Education, conducted an oversight hearing on the employment needs of Amish youth. Representative Souder spoke in support of the exemption. Mr. Souder, representing a partly Amish constituency, explained that those who favor industrial work by children of 14 years of age had not been able to persuade DOL to acquiesce in the practice. Urging a change in the law, Representative Souder argued that the Amish children would be "supervised by adults. who know and care about them" and that the proposed amendment to the FLSA "would protect a truly endangered religion and culture."[11]

Thomas M. Markey, Acting Administrator of the Wage and Hour Division, DOL, also testified concerning employment of Amish youth. He noted that, for reasons of their faith, Amish youth "are exempt from state laws making school attendance compulsory" and, when they have finished the 8th grade and are 14 years of age, they are permitted to work more hours than would normally be the case "and to work during traditional school hours." However, he pointed out: "Sawmills are dangerous places to work, even for adults." Noting the high accident and fatality rates for the industry nationwide, he stated that such work is "even more dangerous for children."[12]

On June 13, 2001, during consideration of S. 1 (the Elementary and Secondary Education Act Authorization), Senator Specter proposed S.Amdt. 420. The Specter amendment would have amended the FLSA to permit Amish youngsters who are over 14 years of age and exempt from compulsory school attendance to work, under specified conditions, in wood products processing. Following an opening statement, a brief colloquy was engaged in between Senators Specter and Kennedy (chair, Committee on Health, Education, Labor, and Pensions). Senator Kennedy affirmed that it "would be valuable to have ...an open hearing" on the issue-particularly with respect to the safety of prospective workers—and agreed that the Committee would conduct such a hearing. At that point, Senator Specter withdrew his

---

[10] This is a *work opportunity* (or *endangerment)* that would not apply with respect to children who are of religions denominations other than Amish and/or certain closely related sects.

[11] Testimony of Representative Mark Souder before the Senate Subcommittee on Labor, Health arid Human Services and Education, Committee on Appropriations, May 3, 2001.

[12] Testimony of Thomas M. Markey, Acting Administrator, Wage and Hour Division, U.S. Department of Labor, before the Subcommittee on Labor, Health and Human Services, and Education, Committee on Appropriations, V.S. Senate, May 3, 2001.

proposed amendment, providing an opportunity for a further hearing on the proposed employment of Amish youth.[13]

On July 25, 2001, legislation to permit Amish youth to work at age 14 in wood processing plants was introduced both in the House and in the Senate: H.R. 2639 (Pitts) and S. 1241 (Specter). No action has been taken on these proposals beyond referral to committee.

---

[13] *Congressional Record,* June 13, 2001, p. 56153-86154.

Chapter 6

LEGISLATING A *LIVING WAGE*

During the past decade, numerous local governments have passed *living wage* statutes and in many other jurisdictions ("more than 70 cities and at least 39 states"), living wage movements are thought to be active.[1] Although these enactments tend to vary from one jurisdiction to the next, they seem most often to (a) set a minimum wage standard higher than the otherwise applicable state or federal wage floor and (b) require that not less than this *local living wage* be paid to persons employed by contractors engaged by the local government or by "employers who receive special treatment from" a city or county.[2] The basic premise of the *living wage* campaign is "that anyone in this country who works for a living should not have to raise a family in poverty."[3]

By the 104th Congress, Representatives Gutierrez and Vento bad introduced legislation (separate and different bills) that would, working from a base of federal contracting, require payment of not less than a living wage: i.e., not less than the federal poverty line for a family of four. Similar bills were introduced in the 105th and 106th Congresses, requiring employers engaged in federal contract work to pay their employees not less than a living wage.

In the 107th Congress, Representative Gutierrez introduced H.R. 917 and H.R. 1457, each titled the "Federal Living Wage Responsibility Age" and which, among other provisions, provide for the following: *First.* The

---

1 While the various "living wage" initiatives are not minimum wage proposals in the traditional sense, they share many of the same purposes.

2 Tolley, George, Peter Bernstein, and Michael Lesage. *Economic Analysis of a Living Wage Ordinance.* Washington, Employment Policies Institute, July 1999, p. 2.

3 Pollin, Robert, and Stephanie Luce. *The Living Wage: Building a Fair Economy.* New York, The New Press, 1998, p. 1.

legislation would set a coverage threshold on federal contract work at $10,000, above which the Act would take effect. *Second.* Under such contracts, workers would have to be paid at a rate "sufficient for a worker to earn, while working 40 hours a week on a fun-time basis, the amount of the Federal poverty level for a family of four." *Third.* Such workers would need to be paid an amount, "determined by the Secretary [of Labor] based on the locality in which a worker resides, sufficient to cover the costs to such worker to obtain any fringe benefits not provided by the worker's employer." The concept of *fringe benefit* is defined in the bill. *Fourth.* Certain small businesses and nonprofit organizations would be exempt from coverage under the act. *Fifth.* The bill provides a section on administration, compliance, and definitions. *Sixth.* The bill provides that the "President may suspend the provisions of this Act in times of emergency." The bills were referred to the Committee on Government Reform and to the Committee on Education and the Workforce.

S. 940 (Dodd), a lengthy umbrella bill, contains a section, "Livable Wages for Employees under Federal Contracts," which is similar to the Gutierrez proposal- but not identical. *Inter alia,* it does not contain the fringe benefit language, and has certain other exemptions and requirements. See also H.R. 1990 (George Miller).

INDEX

#

103rd Congress, 49
104th Congress, 22, 57
105th Congress, 28, 36, 41
106th Congress, vii, 4, 22, 26, 28, 36, 37, 38, 42, 52, 57
107th Congress, v, vii, 1, 5, 9, 21, 22, 23, 27, 28, 32, 35, 36, 38, 39, 41, 47, 48, 50, 57

A

A Bill To Leave No Child Behind, 24
AFL-CIO, 44
agriculture, 14, 25, 50
Alabama, 10
Alaska, 10, 13
American Nurses Association, 46
American Samoa, 9, 10
Amish, viii, 5, 52, 53, 54, 55
Amy Robinson Memorial Act, 51
Arizona, 10
Arkansas, 10

B

bankruptcy, 42
Bureau of Labor Statistics (BLS), 18, 19, 20
Bush, President, 27, 37
Business Week, 22, 23

C

California, 10
Camp Safety Act of 2001, 25
Census Bureau, 48
Chamber of Commerce, 43
child labor, vii, viii, 1, 3, 4, 7, 21, 47, 48, 49, 50, 51, 53
child labor law, viii, 49, 50, 51
child labor protection, vii, 21
child labor regulation, 48, 49
children, 3, 5, 15, 32, 34, 47, 48, 49, 50, 51, 52, 53, 54
Children's Act for Responsible Employment (CARE) Act, 50
civil service, 33, 34
Clinton, President, 4, 22
Colorado, 10
Committee on Energy and Natural Resources, 28

Commonwealth of the Northern Mariana Islands (CNMI), vii, 1, 9, 24, 27, 28
competition, 17, 18, 26
computer services, viii, 37, 39
Congress, iv, vii, 1, 3, 5, 8, 12, 13, 15, 20, 21, 22, 23, 26, 27, 28, 29, 32, 33, 34, 35, 36, 38, 40, 41, 42, 46, 48, 53
Connecticut, 10

D

Delaware, 10
demographic groups, 18
Department of Labor (DOL), vii, 5, 7, 8, 10, 12, 25, 27, 28, 35, 36, 41, 47, 49, 51, 52, 53, 54
Department of Veterans Affairs Medical Programs Enhancement Act of 2001, 46
dependents, 15
disabilities, vii, 25, 28, 29
disabled, 4, 12, 15, 29, 51
District of Columbia, 10, 13

E

Earned Income Tax Credit (EITC), 15, 16, 17
education, 14, 32, 36, 53
elderly, 15
Elementary and Secondary Education Act, 54
employer flexibility, 40
employer rights, 35
Employment Policies Institute, 27, 57
Enhancing Economic Security for America's Working Families Act, 24
ethnicity, 18
exemptions, 3, 4, 7, 16, 17, 58

F

Fair Labor Standards Act (FLSA), i, iii, vii, viii, 1, 3, 4, 5, 7, 8, 9, 10, 11, 13, 14, 16, 17, 21, 22, 23, 24, 25, 26, 27, 28, 29, 31, 32, 33, 34, 35, 36, 37, 38, 39, 40, 41, 42, 44, 45, 47, 49, 50, 51, 53, 54
Fair Labor Standards Act of 1938, 53
families, 15, 17, 23, 24
family income, 15
federal assistance, 12
Federal Living Wage Responsibility Age, 57
federal minimum wage protection, vii, 28
federal workers, 34
Florida, 10
free market, 11, 12

G

Garcia v. San Antonio Metropolitan Transit Authority, 33
Georgia, 10
goods and services, 11, 15, 16
Great Depression, 32, 33
gross volume, 16
Guam, 10

H

H.R. 222, 24
H.R. 546, 24, 36, 39
H.R. 648, 25, 36
H.R. 665, 24, 28
H.R. 881, 25, 29
H.R. 917, 57
H.R. 1441, 27
H.R. 1457, 57
H.R. 1602, 1, 42, 43, 44
H.R. 1869, 51
H.R. 1982, 41

H.R. 1990, 58
H.R. 2070, 1, 25, 39
H.R. 2111, 25
H.R. 2239, 51
H.R. 2241, 24
H.R. 2424, 24
H.R. 2639, 55
H.R. 2679, 25
H.R. 2812, 23, 26
H.R. 3070, 50
H.R. 3238, 45
H.R. 3486, 25
H.R. 3678, 25, 36
Hawaii, 10, 13
hazardous occupation orders (HOs), 49
health insurance, 13
healthcare professionals, 45
Heritage Foundation, 27
hourly paid workers, 18, 19, 20
House Subcommittee on Workforce Protections, 1, 39

I

Idaho, 10
Illinois, 10
immigration laws, 49
immigration policy, 1, 27
income redistribution, 11
Indiana, 10
Insecticide, Fungicide, and Rodenticide Act, 51
inside sales, viii, 1, 38, 39
interstate commerce, 7, 16
Iowa, 10

J

job market, 11

K

Kansas, 10
Kentucky, 10

L

Labor Policy Association (LPA), 35, 43, 44
labor standards, 1, 3, 21, 26, 28, 34, 35, 41, 49, 50
labor standards advocates, 1
labor standards legislation, 1, 21, 26
living wage, 13, 57
Louisiana, 10

M

Maine, 10, 45
market wage, 12
Maryland, 10
Massachusetts, 10
media, 7
Member of Congress, 14
Michigan, 10
minimum wage legislation, 22, 26, 27, 37
minimum wage protections, vii
minimum wage rates, vii, 9, 10
Minimum Wage Restoration Act, 26
minimum wage worker, 12, 13, 14, 15, 17, 18, 19
minimum wage workforce, 14, 17, 18, 20
Minnesota, 10
Mississippi, 10
Missouri, 10
Montana, 10

N

National Industrial Recovery Act (NIRA), 29
Nebraska, 10
Nevada, 10
New Hampshire, 10

New Jersey, 10
New Mexico, 10
New York, iii, iv, 10, 32, 33, 57
North Carolina, 10
North Dakota, 10
Northern Mariana Islands, vii, 28

O

Ohio, 10
Oklahoma, 10
omissions, iv
Oregon, 10
oversight, 33, 34, 39, 54
overtime pay, vii, viii, 1, 3, 4, 7, 25, 27, 31, 32, 34, 35, 36, 37, 38, 39, 40, 44

P

P .L. 104-188, 8, 22, 37
part-time employment, 14
Pennsylvania, 10, 52
per-hour basis, 14
permission, iv
poverty, 12, 15, 57, 58
poverty guidelines, 12
private sector, 33, 34, 40, 41
public agencies, 33
Puerto Rico, 10

R

race, 18
Reagan Administration, 48
regular rate, viii, 1, 3, 4, 31, 41, 42, 44
regular wages, 44
religion, 54
religious faiths, 5
Rhode Island, 10
Roybal-Allard bill, 51

S

S. 1, 28, 42, 46, 54, 55
S. 8, 24, 28, 50, 51
S. 277, 24, 28
S. 507, 1, 28
S. 624, 41
S. 1188, 46
S. 869, 50, 51
S. 940, 24, 28, 58
S. 964, 24, 28
Safe Nursing and Patient Care Act of 2001, 45
sawmills, 5, 52, 53
Secretary of Labor, 8, 9, 28, 29, 48, 50, 51, 52
Senate Committee on Energy and Natural Resources, 1, 28
Small Business Tax Fairness Act of 2001, 25
small businesses, 14, 17, 58
small firms, 4, 16
South Carolina, 10
South Dakota, 10
Specter amendment, 54
statutory minimum wage rate, 29
Subcommittee on Workforce Protections, 1, 35, 42, 53
sub-minimum wage, vii, 12, 14, 17, 18, 22, 25, 29
Supreme Court, 33

T

Tennessee, 10
Texas, 10, 42, 52

U

unemployment, 32
United States, iv, v, 20, 27, 28, 29, 47, 48, 50

United States-Commonwealth of the Northern Marianas Human Dignity Act, 28
Utah, 10

V

Vermont, 10
Virgin Islands, 10
Virginia, 10

W

wage floor, 4, 7, 11, 12, 14, 21, 23, 26, 28, 29, 57
wage rates, 4, 28, 42
Washington, 10, 23, 29, 32, 35, 42, 46, 49, 53, 57
West Virginia, 10
Wisconsin, 10, 32
women, 18, 33, 51, 52
work hours regulation, 4, 32
worker flexibility, 40
Workforce Investment Act of 1998, 51
working mothers, 33
working poor, 10, 11, 21
World War I, 32, 47
World War II, 32, 47
Wyoming, 10

Y

youths, 18, 48

DATE			